HOME

BAPTIST HERITAGE COURSE

PART 2: BAPTISTS IN AMERICA
SCOPE: 16TH CENTURY TO PRESENT

EVANGELIST TED ALEXANDER, D.D.

HOME STUDY EDITION

BAPTIST HERITAGE COURSE

PART 2: BAPTISTS IN AMERICA
SCOPE: 16TH CENTURY TO PRESENT

EVANGELIST TED ALEXANDER, D.D.

Copyright © 2010 Ted Alexander. All rights reserved.

Writings contained herein are by the author unless otherwise stated.

No part of this publication may be reproduced, stored in a retrieval system or transmitted in any way by any means – electronic, mechanical, photocopy, recording or otherwise – without the prior permission of the copyright holder, except as provided by USA copyright law.

All Scriptures are taken from the King James Bible.

ISBN#978-1-935075-88-2

Printed in the United States of America.

Printed by Calvary Publishing
A Ministry of Parker Memorial Baptist Church
1902 East Cavanaugh Road
Lansing, Michigan 48910
www. CalvaryPublishing. org

Acknowledgements

A special thank you goes out to my pastor, Dr. James Beller, whose book *America in Crimson Red* has become the modern day encyclopedia of American Baptist history. This book has been an invaluable resource in the compilation of this study. His continued leadership and support have been a real blessing to the author. "Thank you, Preacher!"

I also want to thank pastors Matthew McPhillips and Joshua Davenport for their continued encouragement. Pastor McPhillips is a faithful proof reader and dear friend. Pastor Davenport was particularly helpful in the area of the various divisions of Baptists in the past 200 years. Evangelist Dewayne Hinson was also "elected" to be a proof reader and editor. Thanks, Friends!

Next, I want to thank my wife for her countless hours of proof reading, editing, typing, and prayers. Anything I have ever accomplished could not have been done without her. Thank you, Honey; I love you!

Lastly, I want to thank the Lord for the glorious history of the church He bled and died for, and for the strength to accomplish this task.

Contents

Lesson One 9
  The Baptists Come to America

Lesson Two 27
  John Clarke and America's First Baptist Church

Lesson Three 47
  Obadiah Holmes and Baptist Persecution in New England

Lesson Four 67
  The Great Awakening

Lesson Five 89
  Shubal Stearns and the Separate Baptists

Lesson Six 109
  Baptists and the American Revolution

Lesson Seven 127
  The Virginia Baptists, a Rare Breed

LESSON EIGHT 149
  American Baptist Missions/American
  Indian Missions

LESSON NINE 171
  The Great Revival of 1800/Baptist
  Expansion

LESSON TEN 187
  Baptist Profiles – Important Pastors,
  Evangelists, Hymn Writers

LESSON ELEVEN 207
  Southern Baptist Convention/Independent
  Baptists

LESSON TWELVE 231
  Baptists in the 21st Century

ANSWER KEYS 251

Lesson One

The Baptists Come to America

But now they desire a better *country*...
Hebrews 11:16a

Ah, America! Even just the sound of the name conjures up thoughts of the great principles which became the pillars of this great nation. When one considers America, it is not very long before the ideals of freedom, liberty, spirituality, bravery, justice, individual rights, and hope come to mind. These grand pillars of principle which describe America have become so common to the average observer that it is feared they are not just simply unappreciated but completely taken for granted. When the liberal university student burns the American flag as those in third-world countries do, it becomes obvious that he is truly ignorant of the great price that was paid to secure the flying of Old Glory. He is misusing a right that was won for him by the very people that he is disrespecting. In like manner, many people have no respect for those who fought for our religious liberty. What sad irony!

It is common knowledge that America is a land

of immigrants. Year after year multiplied waves of immigrants have poured onto America's shores. From English to Scots-Irish, from Germans to Italians, and from Poles to Puerto Ricans, America has been made up of and shaped in many ways by the people who have migrated here. Possibly one of the strangest facts of all is that America has been shaped and influenced in an even greater way, not by a national people group that arrived on her shores, but rather by a religious group. Those people were the Baptists. Although the Baptist Christians are truly from "another country," their strong influence is not in a national identity. The strength of Baptist Christians is in the Lord their God. The change they have made in America, both politically and spiritually, cannot be attributed to something they learned in their mother countries, but is a result of their insistence on using the Bible as their final authority. The principles of God's Word, proclaimed both in life and message by the Baptists, have made their coming to America more important historically than all other people groups, whether religious or secular.

Let the reader be reminded in the strongest of terms that the great, principled foundation on which America was laid was not erected on the sands of chance; nor was it constructed on the same, failed, English platform from which it was severed. America was laid, block by block, document by document, and ideal by ideal on the solid, unchanging bedrock of Baptist principles. These Baptist principles, which are derived from the incomparable Word of God, were carefully set in place by true heroes of liberty. Whether it was the patriot soldier fighting for freedom from an oppressive English government or a Baptist minister unknowingly securing our freedom of conscience as he preached Christ through the bars of a jail cell, America has been great these many years, in part, because it has rested on the stalwart rock of pure, unfeigned liberty. It took imprisonment, humiliation, starvation, stripes, blood, and even death to secure these principles for you and me. This land of liberty has truly been great, and we should thank God for it. But it has not always been so. When your Baptist forebears first placed their feet on this great land, it was obvious that there was much work to be done in order to secure true liberty.

Come along through this lesson as we trace the first, few steps that were necessary in securing liberty and making America one of the most grand and "lively experiments" in the history of mankind. By the end of this lesson it will begin to be clear to the student that every American owes a great debt of gratitude to the Baptists.

The Old Country

Before a just treatise on Baptist migration to the "New World" can be properly conveyed, several issues must be thrown into the discussion and duly considered. The information necessary to understand Baptist migration shall be ascertained as a result of the reader considering several questions. These questions are as follows:

1. Why did the Baptists come to America?
2. Where did they come from?
3. When did they come?
4. What was their motherland like?
5. What were the circumstances surrounding their journey to the still futuristic "Land of the Free?"

These questions will all be answered before the conclusion of lesson one. In short, the old country must be studied to understand the new. The American historian, Clarence B. Carson, stated it this way:

> "The importance of the European background for explaining the United States can hardly be exaggerated. The United States derives from and is an extension of Western civilization. The center of that civilization has long been western Europe…"

(Clarence B. Carson. *A Basic History of the United*

States, Vol. 1: The Colonial Experience, 1607-1774, p. 9.)

One might ask, "What does this have to do with the Baptists?" The answer is: what makes America a great land of liberty and a political role model throughout the world is our biblical Baptist principles. But the struggle here over principles was just a continuation of a long time struggle; a struggle cruelly transplanted here from Europe, and more specifically from England. The most hated of all the freedom fighting dissenters in the old country were none other than the Baptists. Now let's cross the ocean and visit the memory of our Baptist forefathers in the old country!

Europe's Atrocity: The Marriage of Governmental Powers and Religious Hierarchies

The vast majority of early Baptist migrants came here from England. England's royal heads acted as religious directors, enforcers, and persecutors. Although there were diverse religious affiliations among England's leaders through the 1500s and 1600s, the one glaring constant was oppression and persecution of all who dared to think and act freely concerning religious matters.

Full religious liberty was unheard of. Consider

the following examples. The English leaders trampled on the consciences of men.

Henry VIII (1509-1547) In 1529, this man established the autonomous Church of England by pulling it out of the Roman Catholic Church. The main reason he did so was to make the church his slave. Henry desired a divorce and was denied that request by the Pope. The church's subservience to this worldly man was exemplified in the fact that the newly formed Anglican body granted their founder his petition of divorce.

Mary I (1553-1558) She enforced Catholic dogma on the populace. Her persecution of dissenters and overall harsh treatment of her subjects earned her the famed title of "Bloody Mary."

Elizabeth I (1558-1603) She despised the papacy once venerated by Queen Mary. Instead she favored the Episcopal Church of England. She persecuted dissenters; and during her reign, the often times blood-thirsty Catholics were oppressed and persecuted. Over two hundred Catholics were put to death under her reign. Non-Catholics who disagreed with Elizabeth were imprisoned for the first offence, banished for the second offence, and if they returned were put to death.

James I (1603-1625) The Puritans in England who hoped to find relief under James were sadly mistaken. James had ruled Scotland before coming to England, and the Puritans of England held many views similar to Scotland's Presbyterian population. For this reason, they expected sympathy from the king. However, James established and broadcast his philosophy of government-church marriage early in his tenure. His famous statement was, "No bishop, no king." He meant that unless a hierarchy ruled the church it would be difficult for a hierarchy to rule the state. James prevented dissenters from leaving England to worship freely. He further confiscated goods. He humiliated and imprisoned all who disagreed with his church-state philosophy.

Charles I (1625-1649) He made William Laud, archbishop of Canterbury, the religious head of the Church of England. Laud was an evil man who enforced a strict Anglicanism and attempted to monitor the churches for any Puritan or Baptist views or writings that disagreed with Anglicanism. During these years many people were burned at the stake.

Charles II (1660-1685) The historian J. R. Graves stated that Charles II was "an Episcopalian by profession but a Papist at heart." He passed the Act of Uniformity as an attempt to force all his subjects to conform to and support the Episcopal Church. There were some ministers who compromised for the sake of their welfare and that of their families. But there were others who were led by principles and, like the apostle Paul of old, were beaten, had all their worldly goods confiscated, and were imprisoned. There, in those dark prisons, an untold number perished standing for Jesus Christ.

This was the climate in England for centuries, and of all those persecuted there was one body of believers that saw much greater persecution than all the rest, the Baptists. The Lord's true scriptural churches were more hated, misunderstood and maligned than all other groups put together.

Examples of Baptist Persecution in England

It has already been pointed out in volume one of this study that the vast majority of great Anabaptist leaders in the sixteenth and seventeenth centuries were cruelly martyred. Balthaser Hubmaier was burned at the stake in 1528, Felix Manz was drowned in 1527, George Blaurock was burned in 1529, Michael Sattler was cruelly tortured in an unthinkable manner and then burned in 1527; but this is truly just the tip of the iceberg. Upon studying these Anabaptist leaders and their deaths, one must be careful not to think that persecution was limited to the countries of Germany and Switzerland. England also saw horrible persecution which defied all human compassion.

Did Bloody Mary hate your Baptist forefathers?
She hated them enough not only to burn them,

but she also despised the thought of their decomposing corpses, seemingly at rest, buried in the ground in England. She, in accordance with the wicked Catholic practice of many Bible-haters down through the years, proceeded to dig up the corpses of those who were discovered to be Anabaptists after their death. In one specific instance, a man named David George had his corpse exhumed and burnt three years after it was buried. The Baptist historian Ray records the following in his book on Baptist succession:

> "Fourteen women and a youth were put on board a vessel and sent out of the country. The youth was whipped from the prison to the wharf. Five others were consigned to Newgate, where they were put in heavy irons, thrust into a damp and filthy dungeon, swarming with vermin and not allowed to associate with other prisoners, lest the thieves and murderers in the jail should be corrupted by Anabaptist contamination!"

One of these in prison died eight days later.

Was King James a friend to the Baptists?
Ironically, the same year his authorized Bible was completed, 1611, he burned a man alive for supposedly denying the doctrine of the Trinity. The following year, King James burned the Baptist Edward

Wightman alive. Thomas Crosby wrote, *"If Wightman really held all the opinions laid to his charge, he must have been an idiot or a madman, and ought to have had the prayers of his persecutors…"*

In 1646, Samuel Oats, a Baptist preacher, was arrested and put in irons for murder. The charge stated that a woman he immersed died a few weeks later. While in court, however, the truth came out. It was shown that after her baptism, she was actually in better health than she had been in for a considerable period of time.

It is common knowledge among Baptists that our great forefather John Bunyan, author of the much loved *Pilgrim's Progress*, was imprisoned in Bedford jail and suffered there for twelve years. His crime — he was a Baptist and could not but preach Baptist doctrine.

As our final example of the sufferings of Baptists in England, we submit the following:

> "In 1661, Elder John James was hung and quartered in England by order of Charles II for his Baptist principles. His quarters were placed over the city gates, in London, and his head was set upon a pole at the meeting house in which he had preached the Gospel" (taken from Shackelford's *Compendium of Baptist History*).

The previous facts are representative of the religious climate of Europe, and specifically England, toward our Baptist forebears. It would be impossible to record in a volume this size the complete record that is available on this subject. The author feels as J. A. Wylie must have felt when he wrote concerning the ancient Baptists and their sufferings. He said, *"Thus the roll of martyrs runs on, and with each new sufferer comes a new, a more excruciating and more horrible mode of death and torture."*

This is the England that sent our Baptist fathers fleeing to America in hope of a new life - a life of liberty to serve God from the heart.

Great Expectations

The Baptist people are a people of hope. Baptist Christians are commanded to be, "Looking for that blessed hope…" It was with this spiritual mindset that many Baptists began to sail in search of religious liberty. Sure there were others who longed to be free, but none had a history as long, sad and bloody as the Baptists. The centuries-long struggle for liberty of conscience was a nagging fact to Baptists throughout the ages. From the beheading of the first Baptist through the Waldensian persecutions and on to England's awful burning stakes, the Baptists had to endure Satan's best attempts to exterminate them. However, with no history of Catholic or

Anglican strong-arm rule in the New World, expectations were somewhat high that this place could be somewhat of a "promised land" for men who longed to be free in their hearts. As ships began to leave for America, the oppressed looked on, only dreaming of a place where they could have their own churches and ministers. In short order, God's providence would allow for handfuls of Baptists to be passengers aboard ships to America.

Shock

While on their journeys to America, Baptists, Pilgrims, Quakers, and other dissenting groups engaged in intriguing conversations. What they learned in these talks was disturbing news, to say the least. Could it be possible that the new country which would have as its inhabitants many Puritans, Baptists, Pilgrims, and Quakers, would quickly become a place of betrayal? Could a country starting from scratch become a wretched, disgraceful land of ecclesiastical coercion and enforced religious laws and taxes? Surely it would have to be a place where all men worshipped freely. Surely the Puritans, being once persecuted themselves, could never become oppressors, could they?

The following narrative is taken from the book *Trials and Sufferings for Religious Liberty in New England* by Baptist historian J. R. Graves. Consider the

Lesson One

words of this quote and try to understand just how badly these noble Baptists hoped for the "best" in the "new" England.

> "All the people do not submit. Our being on board this vessel today is the proof, and the consequence, that we will not submit. No man, whether priest, archbishop, or king, shall coerce my religious views."
>
> "No man or men, neither kings nor kings' ministers, conferences nor assemblies of ministers have a right to make laws for Christians," said Mr. Fairbanks, and raising himself to his full height, "I tell you, sir, Christ is the Christians only king."
>
> "But are you certain that the colonial government in America will not interfere with your theological views?"
>
> "How can they? They know the evil of it. Persecution has driven them from their own land. It would be the most palpable inconsistency for them to inflict upon others that from which they have fled themselves."
>
> "So it seems to me," said Stephen. "They would be as bad as their persecutors, for they would be guilty of similar conduct."

As the student will see, the hopeful Baptists were in for great disappointment upon their arrival in America. This will be fully discussed in the ensuing lessons.

Struggling and Settling: The State-Church Mentality Woefully Transplanted

It must be either human nature or simply common sense to expect that those who have struggled would sympathize with others who are struggling. We would expect those who were once poor or oppressed to find it in their hearts to be kind to others facing similar circumstances. The sad reality is that all of this is just wishful thinking. The once persecuted Puritans, upon their arrival in the New World, seemed to have forgotten their own history. They were at one time, not so long before, disfranchised, banished, and even burned along with the dissenting Baptists. This, however, made no difference to most of the Puritan leaders. As soon as the chance was afforded them, they very quickly set up their own state-church.

Read and discuss the following quote from Dr. James Beller's book, *America in Crimson Red*:

> A real understanding of our republic must begin with an understanding of these pioneering Englishmen who came seeking a better country...The Puritans have a horrific record concerning the baptized believers. The Puritans came to American shores to escape the brutality and persecuting arm of the

notorious Church of England henchman—William Laud. And with freedom theirs, the reformed children of Rome were faced with the same question that dogged Luther and Calvin: Where does the authority of "the Church" begin and end? Would the New World have a feudal government and religious establishment, or civil government and religious liberty? Sadly our Puritan forefathers chose the former for New England. John Callender alluded that these first Americans were incapable of "mutual forbearance" and their religious intolerance would last into the 19th century.

The Baptists were faced with intolerance, but they stayed in their new homeland to carve out religious liberty, stripe by stripe and imprisonment by imprisonment!

Review Questions

1. America's grand pillars of principle are completely _____ for _____.

2. America is a land of _____.

3. The most influential group to ever immigrate to America was the _____.

4. The strength of Baptist Christians is in the _____ _____ _____.

5. America owes a great _____ _____ _____ to the Baptists.

6. The importance of the _____ _____ for explaining the United States can hardly be exaggerated.

7. The struggle here over principles was just a _____ _____ ___ _____ _____ struggle.

8. The vast majority of early Baptist migrants came here from _____.

9. England's royal heads acted as _____ _____, _____, and _____.

10. England's leaders trampled on the _____ of men.

Lesson One

Fill in the blanks with the proper name of England's leaders.

11. _____ This man established the autonomous Church of England.

12. _____ She despised the papacy and even persecuted Catholics.

13. _____ He made William Laud his chief murderer.

14. _____ She enforced the laws of Romanism and earned the name "Bloody Mary."

15. _____ He made the statement, "No bishop, no king."

16. _____ Graves said this man was "an Episcopalian by profession but a Papist at heart."

True or False

17. _____ Bloody Mary spared the Baptists but killed Puritans.

18. _____ John Bunyan spent 12 months in prison.

19. _____ Elder John James held to Puritan principles.

20. _____ When the first Baptists left for America, they went to start a state church.

Lesson Two

John Clarke and America's First Baptist Church

> And so were the churches established in the faith, and increased in number daily.
>
> **Acts 16:5**

God in His providence has allowed many great men and women to be used as framers, founders, and even fighters for truth and right. Few men excel in more than one of these fields. A handful of men have understood the immense importance of both religious and civil liberty and their relationship to one another. An even more obscure company of good men have championed religious and civil liberty while showing men the liberty of soul that only comes through a born again experience with Jesus Christ. A mostly unknown New England Baptist minister of the 17th century was one such man! If ever a list could be compiled that contained the names of the most important men in America's history, as well as the world's history, this man's name would most surely appear near the very top. His name is Dr. John Clarke.

For those who think the previous statements are

more like overstatements, consider just a few of the many accomplishments of John Clarke. Dr. Clarke started the first Baptist church on American soil, which he pastored for thirty-eight years. He held the first recorded evangelistic revival meeting in the New World. He was honored after his death for his medical contributions by the Newport Medical Society. He was the author of the *Portsmouth Compact*. He was the procurer of the famous *Colonial Charter of 1663*. In addition to all of these accomplishments, he was a deputy governor for two terms, a deputy in the assembly for some years, and a chief commissioner in adjusting the boundaries of the land. If this is not enough, he was elected to codify the laws and later to compose and organize the statutes of his colony. This is not all he did, but let it suffice to prove to the greatest skeptic that Dr. John Clarke is most worthy of great attention in a volume such as this.

Many in the unsaved world marvel at his life of accomplishments. How much more should Baptists be well acquainted with and appreciative of all that he was and did! This lesson will outline Clarke's life and demonstrate how important his contributions to liberty and Christianity truly were.

The Pivotal, Dr. John Clarke

In the course of human history, twists and turns

that change the entire landscape of the world are clearly evident. The founding of the nation of Israel, the somewhat recent rebirth of Israel, the rise and fall of Rome, and the climb and subsequent "crash and burn" of Nazi Germany are just a few of those hinge-type events. In the last millennium, however, the most important human event concerning the nations has been the creation of America, the land of liberty. America, with all of her flaws, has yielded enormous influence throughout the entire world. Much of this influence has been positive. The distribution of millions of Bibles, tracts, tons of food, and democratic ideals are just a few of the ways the existence of America has shaped world history. When God set out to unfold His plan for an America, He chose to raise up key men whom He could use to unfold the plan and paint the new landscape. John Clarke was such a man. He was absolutely raised up for "such a time as this." The author often refers to him as the pivotal John Clarke. And why call him this? Everything he did was either revolutionary, unheard of, or was simply thought to be impossible. Yet the tasks he accomplished, to Clarke, seemed to be only his "reasonable service." He ministered in an era where the first building blocks were laid politically, spiritually, and physically. It is not an exaggeration to say that he was a church builder, a colony builder, and a key early framer of our sound form of government itself. In our next section, we will examine these three areas under the heading of "The Pioneering Clarke." For now, let's examine his background information.

His Birth

John Clarke was born on October 3, 1609, in the small farming community of Westhorpe, England. He was reared in a family of eight children. Five of his siblings followed him to the New World, where four of them settled at Newport.

His Education and Expertise

He attended his local village school and would later attend the University of Leyden in Holland. One can only assume, having no clear record, that even in his formative years Clarke was a scholar by every definition. By the time he landed in America, he was not just acquainted with several fields of learning but literally mastered them all. He was a master in theology. He caused the learned heathen of his day to stutter and second guess themselves when he opened his mouth in defense of the Baptist faith. There were more than a few religious leaders and state officials who regretted undertaking a public debate with him.

His skills in medicine were equally incredible. True believers should understand why. It should be a common conviction among believers that those who know the "Great Physician" are most qualified to take upon them the task of healing the sick. As has already been stated, "He was honored after his death for his medical contributions by the Newport Medical Society."

Not only did he excel in these areas, but he also had a firm grasp on the principles of law. Clarke was not just the average lawyer. He focused his knowledge of the law toward the one area he was most well known for his expertise as a statesman and framer of civil government. When one considers just how brilliant a mind he possessed and the many difficult fields he excelled in, one is dumbfounded. In wisdom alone, history struggles to produce an equal to Brother John Clarke.

The Pioneering Dr. John Clarke

John Clarke has a list of accomplishments that cannot be fully examined in just a few short pages. Some of these accomplishments have been listed in the introductory paragraph of this lesson. We will now focus on the two areas where he made the greatest impact.

Church Builder

We realize that the Bible clearly teaches that Jesus Christ has promised to build His church. This truth is found in Matthew 16:18. God is sovereign and He deserves all the glory for promising and performing this task. Yet when it comes to building much needed facilities for His churches to meet in, He delegates such labors to faithful men. The actual gathering, organizing, teaching, and preaching duties are also committed to God's men. Faithful men work for God and with God and are blessed by God to accomplish great things. Clarke was a tool that God used to transplant Baptist principles and practices, as well as scriptural authority, into the New World. He would not be the only one to come and spread his Baptist faith; many would follow. He was, however, the first to do so. Amazingly, the labors he performed produced a congregation that has perpetually met in Newport for nearly four hundred years. This is a testimony, not only of Clarke's willingness to serve, but also of God's willingness to use sinful man.

Clarke's Arrival Opens His Eyes to the Need

John Clarke landed in the New World in 1637. There in Boston, he, along with his wife Elizabeth, began to minister to the needs of the people. Initially, his skill as a doctor was of utmost importance, as doctors were scarce and sickness was common in those days.

It wasn't long before Clarke became a lightning

rod of disruption and protest. Clarke very quickly became aware of the sad facts concerning the churches of New England. Roger Williams had been banished before Clarke ever arrived. Subsequently, the "magistrate's law" was passed. This law made it illegal to be affiliated with "non-approved" churches.

Debate and Division

During this time, there was debate in the air. The Antinomian debates involved the truths of law and grace. These debates began as discussions as to what evidence is accepted as proof of salvation. They evolved into full-blown bones of contention and ultimately harsh division. The Antinomians were the preachers of grace and were within the bounds of sound theology in this particular debate. Even the most scriptural of the Congregational preachers were quickly banished or persuaded to embrace the errors of the establishment churches.

During this time, a woman named Anne Hutchison, an Antinomian, was ex-communicated from the church. In March of 1638, the Reverend John Wilson, standing in his "crow's nest" pulpit, publicly stated these words:

> Therefore, in the name of the Lord Jesus Christ and in the name of the Church I do not only pronounce you worthy to be cast out, but I do cast you out; and

in the name of Christ do I deliver you up to Satan, that you may learn no more to blaspheme, to seduce and to lie; and I do account you from this time forth to be a Heathen and a Publican, and so to be held of all the brethren and sisters of this congregation and of others; therefore, I command you in the name of Christ Jesus and of the church as a leper to withdraw yourself out of the congregation

(*The Hero of Aquidneck: A Life of Dr. John Clarke* by Wilbur Nelson).

Many others were disfranchised, excommunicated, or met similar fates. Clarke himself was without a gun, as his weapons had been confiscated for suspicion of Anabaptism.

The First Baptist Church
Both the need to relocate and to organize a scriptural church were pressing on the heart of Brother Clarke. And so, being the leader that he was, he tackled both issues at the same time. He would prove to be founder not only of a place to exist, but founder and leader of a scriptural, New Testament congregation ordered after the laws of God's Holy Word.

The first Baptist congregation in America existed in its infant form by the winter of 1637. Clarke's family and eighteen other families traveled to New

Hampshire at this time in search of religious liberty. The group that left Boston, being so zealously involved in their form of religious teachings, surely must have had organized preaching services even as they were on the move. We, admittedly, have no concrete evidence that Clarke organized them into a church and administered scriptural ordinances at this time; however, knowing his enterprising spirit, strong Baptist convictions, his desire to be Biblical, and his future faithful service, we assume this traveling congregation was properly ordered. It is the belief of many that Clarke was baptized and ordained in Elder Stillwell's church in London, England.

This group of travelers would not find rest in New Hampshire and were thus forced to move. The move from Boston was to flee the hot debates, whereas the move from New Hampshire was to flee the cold winter. In early 1638, they traveled on southward and into the Narragansett Bay. Here, freedom fighter Roger Williams coaxed them to move on to the island of Aquidneck, and this they did.

Before long, they landed on the island that would eventually be called "Rhode Island." The year was 1638. They purchased this piece of land from the Indians and settled on its northern section. This little dot on a map, which they called Portsmouth, is where the famous *Portsmouth Compact* authored by Clarke was signed. The traveling group landed and immediately compacted together to form a government with full liberty of conscience for all. This truly was a landmark event.

Still in 1638, a portion of this original group, including Clarke, migrated to a little piece of ground on the south end of the island. They named the place Newport. Not only was Newport founded at this time, but it became the permanent home for the first Baptist church. This congregation, started and pastored at the first by Clarke, still exists today in Newport.

Note of interest: The church Clarke started is now named the United Baptist John Clarke Memorial Church. The author has had the privilege of visiting and studying this church, and highly recommends it as a great place to visit in order to partake in some excellent "living history."

Colony Builder

The legal, political, and diplomatic work that John Clarke engaged in would eventually aid in the establishment of a colony. This colony would, in time, become the state of Rhode Island. From the very first days of Clarke's arrival in Boston, his incredible influence in political happenings was felt throughout the New World. He, for many years, held ideas that few others did. He knew how to articulate these great principles, and the effects were far reaching. His political involvement must not be understood as some sort of strong-armed manipulation. Rather, he was ever the diplomat and gentleman. His whole reason for leaving Boston was to establish a church in a country where he and others could peaceably worship the Lord. Unlike the Anglicans, he never had a desire to rule the hearts and minds of men.

The Baptist pastor, Dr. Wilbur Nelson, said the following about Clarke's work as a statesman:

> From the beginning of the movement that resulted in the founding of Portsmouth and Newport until the charter of 1663 was obtained, he was active in public affairs. He held few public offices but served on many important committees, and in a wise and constructive way was the advisor and leading spirit in the organization and administration of town and colony government.

Active Public Servant

The political labors of Clarke were done with virtually selfless motives. As we will see, the results of his work and blessings of his sacrifice would be enjoyed much more by future generations than even his own generation.

Portsmouth Compact

To the casual observer, Portsmouth, Rhode Island, appears to be a common everyday northeastern town. The truth is that here is where America had its first taste of true, unbridled liberty! The traveling group landed here, and Clarke drew up a governmental compact to live by. The compact reads as follows:

Portsmouth Compact

We, whose names are underwritten, do hereby solemnly in the presence of Jehovah incorporate ourselves into a bodie Politick and, as He shall help, will submit our persons, lives and estates unto our Lord Jesus Christ, the King of Kings, and Lord of Lords, and to all those perfect and absolute laws of His given in His Holy Word of truth, to be guided and judged thereby.

Memorial Stone and Tablet

The compact was then signed by twenty three of the leading men in the group.

This bronze tablet, attached to a large stone, was unveiled in 1936 in memory of the unique accomplishment of John Clarke and his friends. It reads:

> Erected to honor the memory and perpetuate the spirit and ideals of the Founders of the first government in the world to allow and to insure its citizens civil and religious liberty. Established on this site in 1638.

As great as this was, it was only the first step in Clarke's establishing a larger group of people on an even larger piece of land under the same governing principles of liberty of conscience.

The Colonial Charter

In the Rhode Island State House in Providence, framed in an expensive fire-proof safe, is housed one of the most uniquely important documents ever produced in the history of the world. This document granted "a full liberty in religious concernments" to the people of Rhode Island. *The Rhode Island Charter*, sometimes referred to as the *Colonial Charter of 1663*, was authored and won virtually single-handedly by none other than Dr. John Clarke. This ancient document, beautifully penned on fine parchment, should be studied, modeled, and appreciated by individuals and governments throughout the world.

Carved into the marble above the south entrance of the Providence State House are the following words taken from the charter itself: *"To—Hold—Forth—A—Lively—Experiment—That—A—Most—Flourishing—Civil—State—May—Stand—And—Best—Be—Maintained—With—Full—Liberty—In—Religious—Concernments."* The previous principles are what Clarke called, "a lively experiment." These words, "lively experiment," have been often quoted as a description of this experimental form of government framed by Clarke.

The procuring of this document was not a task for the unconcerned or commonplace citizen. Once again, as the divine hand of grace moved, this hand directed John Clarke to sacrifice a large part of his life to win a right for the Gospel to be freely preached among the people of the colonies. By the time 1663 rolled around, Clarke had spent a total of thirteen years as an ambassador sent from Rhode Island. His sole purpose was to persuade the Crown, through much diplomacy and scholarly evidence, that there was a great need for liberty of conscience in the New World. In 1652, Clarke wrote his famous book entitled *Ill Newes from New England*. In this book he proclaimed the mistreatment of the Baptist brethren in the New World. One popular statement in this book reads as such: "While Old England is becoming new, New England is becoming old." This burden Clarke carried and this burden he pleaded until Charles II granted him the charter in 1663.

Importance and Influence of the Charter

This charter was the ruling document in Rhode Island until the colony became a state; and then it became the state constitution for another sixty-seven years. The present-day state constitution was adopted in 1843 and holds much of the same principles the original charter did. The original colonial charter was then retired.

For one hundred eighty years, these principles governed the state of Rhode Island and Providence Plantations.

> Thomas Jefferson is said to have given Dr. John Clarke the credit for obtaining this remarkable charter, and to have named it as one of the sources from which he derived the principles of the Declaration of Independence (Nelson, pg. 62).

The Praiseworthy Dr. John Clarke

The unsung hero: The sad reality is that many have never heard of John Clarke or his great principles. His sacrificial life is a narrative that begs to be heralded to the next generation as well as to the present one. He is one of history's most unsung heroes. Wilbur Nelson, writing in the preface of *The*

Hero of Aquidneck, said this of Clarke, "The magnitude of his life and labors has never been fully appreciated." Nelson went on to say,

> Dr. John Clarke of Newport was one of the most eminent men of the seventeenth century. No name in the annals of American history is more important than his, no character deserving of more lasting honor. As a Christian gentleman, pure-minded, unselfish, modest and sincere, he represents the noblest type of American manhood. As a scholar, physician and Christian minister, he takes high rank. As a statesman, laboring to establish a commonwealth on the principle of a "full liberty in religious concernments," he has been properly called "the foremost American diplomat of his age." Loved and admired by his fellow citizens, he was *The Hero of Aquidneck.*

**John Clarke receiving the
Rhode Island Charter of 1663**
(Artist rendering, commissioned by the Baptist History Preservation Society)

Lesson Two

C. E. Barrows stated this of Dr. John Clarke:

From its inception, Mr. Clarke was a leading spirit in the new colony. His life is so interwoven with its history that to have a correct knowledge of the one necessitates a knowledge of the other. He was almost always employed for the public good. His disciplined mind brought constant and invaluable aid to the infant colony. To no one, perhaps, was the colony under greater obligations than to him. Yet so quietly and unobtrusively did he do his work that his great merits have not been duly appreciated. But the careful student of this early period discovers in him the colony's guiding genius. The better his history is known, the more commanding is the position assigned him.

We find that his own contemporaries thought fondly of him. The great freedom fighter Roger Williams wrote the following concerning Clarke in the flyleaf of one of his books: "For his honored and beloved Mr. John Clarke, an eminent witness of Jesus Christ agst ye bloodie Doctrine of persecution" (written in *Bloody Tenent Yet More Bloody*).

Again, C. E. Barrows is quoted as saying, *"[He] deserve[s] to be enrolled among the benefactors of the world."*

Review Questions

1. Dr. Clarke started the first _____ _____ on American soil, which he pastored for thirty-eight years.

2. Dr. Clarke held the first recorded _____ _____ meeting in the New World.

3. Dr. Clarke was the author of the _____ Compact.

4. Dr. Clarke was the procurer of the famous _____ _____ of 1663.

5. Dr. Clarke was a _____ _____ for two terms.

6. Many in the unsaved world marvel at his life of _____.

7. Everything Clarke did was either _____, unheard of, or was simply thought to be _____.

8. Clarke was born in the small farming community of Westhorpe, _____.

9. Even in his formative years, Clarke was a _____ by every definition.

10. Clarke caused the learned heathen of his day to _____ and second guess themselves when he opened his mouth in defense of the Baptist faith.

11. The "_____ law" was passed. This law made it illegal to be affiliated with "_____-_____" churches.

12. The _____ debates involved the truths of law and grace.

13. Clarke's family and eighteen other families left Boston and traveled to _____ _____ in search of religious liberty.

14. The first Baptist congregation in America existed in its _____ form by the winter of 1637.

15. It is the belief of many that Clarke was baptized and ordained in Elder _____ church in _____, _____.

16. The church Clarke started is now named the United Baptist _____ _____ _____ Church.

17. The Rhode Island Charter is housed in the State House in _____, Rhode Island.

18. The charter is framed in an expensive _____-_____ safe.

19. Clarke had spent a total of _____ years as an ambassador sent from Rhode Island.

20. Nelson said that Clarke was "one of the most _____ men of the seventeenth century."

Bonus: C. E. Barrows is quoted as saying, "[He] deserve[s] to be enrolled among the _____ of the world."

Lesson Three

Obadiah Holmes and
Baptist Persecution in New England

Thou therefore endure hardness, as a good soldier of Jesus Christ.

2 Timothy 2:3

As the baptized believers in New England began to multiply so did their enemies. The enemies of religious liberty have always been around. However, it may shock many Baptists today to discover the magnitude of Baptist sufferings right here in America. We often think of Italy, France, and Switzerland when we consider Baptist persecution. In lesson three we are going to uncover one of the most forgotten tragedies of all time, Baptist persecution in New England. The tragedy of Baptist suffering in America is magnified by the ironic fact that it was carried out mostly by those who professed to be "Christians." We understand that practicing Catholics are mostly unsaved individuals. We can see in history where even popes have differentiated between Catholic and Christians. To this distinction we agree. But to understand Baptist persecution in

New England it is important to remember that, unlike the Catholics of by-gone centuries, a substantial percentage of the Puritan persecutors had made clear professions of faith in Christ. Only God knows how many were truly saved; however, it is safe to say that there were, at times, Puritan Christians persecuting Baptist Christians. It is interesting to note that a clear record of the opposite cannot be found anywhere. Baptists, by their very core principles, could not persecute others for a religious conviction of any sort. This is because Baptists have a holy conviction that men must be left alone to freely accept Christ by no other convincement than that by which the Holy Ghost may bring about through the preached Word. True Baptists also allow for individuals to reject Christ if they insist on doing so.

The Puritans of New England did not believe in soul liberty. To grasp this truth is simple when one begins to understand what a Puritan is. Puritans were simply people who wanted to purify the Church of England. Instead of separating from Anglicanism like the Pilgrims, they chose to stay underneath its corrupt umbrella and to attempt to steer it in the right direction. An attempt to steer Anglicanism in the right direction, for the Puritans, was kin to trying to bail out the Titanic after striking the iceberg; it simply was not going to happen. Puritans maintained compulsory infant baptism.

The Puritans required religious taxes to support the local parish. They imprisoned, disfranchised, beat, and banished all non-conformists.

When Baptists start to learn the truth about early American Puritanism, it begins to open up a huge can of worms. Many questions beg to be answered. For starters: why were we taught that the Puritans were all kind, loving people who never bothered a fly? Why were we taught that Puritans championed the principles of religious liberty? These are just a few pieces of history that have been portrayed in a light that would make Puritanism look good.

We will now lay out the case against Puritanism. Their religious heresy will be exposed and their principles will be compared and contrasted with the Bible. True liberty was won in America; however, the only part Puritanism had in it was to become a hindrance and a stumbling block to liberty. God Himself would then intervene and use the Baptists to establish biblical principles in this great land. To be sure, the religious liberty enjoyed in America today can be traced to great statesmen like John Clarke and Roger Williams. But there were also great men who deserve much credit and yet never stood before kings and dignitaries. Comparatively, these men may seem less important in the grand scheme of things. It is important to remember that America did not become great simply because of diplomacy or worldly intelligence. Often times it was resistance, civil disobedience, bold, public preaching, and other grassroots efforts that pushed back at the established church authority. We have in our Baptist lineage men of toughness and renown. Such a man was Obadiah Holmes. His untold story will be thoroughly examined in this lesson.

Baptist Principles of Liberty vs. the State Church Machine

As has been stated, Baptists in New England championed the cause for a limited civil government. The New England Baptists did not believe it was the role of the state to be involved in religious affairs, except for its protection of the right of free exercise of religion. Both John Clarke and Roger Williams believed that the state should not attempt to enforce the "first table" of the law. The first table was the first four commandments. Because these commandments deal with man's relationship to God, both Clarke and Williams felt that the state should not meddle in these affairs. They believed that the state's responsibility was to oversee the enforcement of the second table of the law. The second table is the last six commandments. These commandments deal with man's relationship to man. Because of the nature of the second table, the New England Baptists agreed that it fell under legitimate state jurisdiction.

Lesson Three

The Calvinist Theocracy

The Puritans were Calvinists. Because of this theological error, they believed in covenant theology. Covenant theology is a system whereby Israel is completely done away with and is replaced completely by the church. This is also called replacement theology. The Puritans believed that since Israel was a theocracy and had a government responsible to enforce both tables of the law, then the church should function in the same way. They said that circumcision was the seal of the covenant in old times, and in like manner baptism is the new entry door into covenant relationship with God today. This is why infant baptism was insisted upon. Covenant theologians are not looking for the return of the Lord. The theological system they embrace teaches men that the "church" is presently ushering in the kingdom. This can only work if the "church" is married to the state. Often-times this system of error is caped in the fancy name of reformed theology. Make no mistake, reformed means hyper-Calvinistic. The vast majority of the "religious right" embraces this error and therefore calls the biblical separation of church and state a fallacy! They are wrong!

A Garden

The New England Baptists resisted tyranny while demanding upon a proper separation of church and state. Williams, a professed Baptist for a time and long-time friend of Baptists and liberty, spoke of a "wall of separation" (This can be found in *Roger Williams: His Contribution to American Tradition*, by Perry Miller 1962). Williams used the biblical analogy of a "garden enclosed" for the church. He further said that the state was the wilderness outside the garden. This was the same belief to which Baptists through the ages held. Rome's state-church monstrosity was opposed by the Baptists throughout the Dark Ages because Baptists have always believed in a separation of church and state.

False Teaching on the Separation of Church and State

Error on the Left — Many people today have bought the lie that there should be no influence on the state whatsoever by the church. To disprove this theory, one has to look no further than the words of the founding fathers themselves. George Washington said, *"It is impossible to rightly govern the world without God and the Bible."* The proofs of the influence of Christianity on our early government can be seen in many other similar statements. The influence of Christianity and the Bible can be seen in the founding documents and traditional Christian practices in our government. There is no doubt that both, the God of the Bible and our forefathers, believed that the church should shed its righteous light on the state. Today's modern attempt to erase all references to God, all religious symbols, prayers, and other Christian influences, is a slap in the face of our fore-fathers. To act like our founders were all atheists and wanted God erased from society and government is a horrible example of humanism running its course. That being said, it is imperative to note that our framers did not want religion to rule the state. They envisioned a balance at work. A separation of church and state was the key to this just balance.

Error on the Right — Many today believe it is a lie to declare that there is a separation of church and state. We can clearly see, however, that when there is not a proper separation, state-churches begin to appear, and they become monstrous entities of persecution. They attempt to force men to conform to their false views under threat of punishment. Thomas Jefferson referenced this separation in the famed "Danbury Letter." The religious right is running around hollering to all who will listen that there is no such thing as separation of church and state, and that this is a fictitious belief. The reason they feel this way is because they, like the Puritans, are Calvinists. The religious right is not governed by biblical, Baptist principles. They espouse dominion theology. The religious right is made up of theocrats and replacement theologians. Quite frankly, it is understandable why the liberals are scared to death of the religious right. Given half a chance, they would no doubt set up a state church again, as this is what their theology dictates.

Think About It — Can you imagine standing at the jail cell of one of the early Baptist preachers in America? There he sits, put in jail by the state-church. He has lost his home, his job, his congregation, and his freedom. How do you think he will respond when you remind him that the separation of church and state is just a myth? If he reaches through the jail bars after you, don't wonder why. There must be a proper separation of the two entities.

Baptists Have the Correct Understanding
Sadly, the ones with the balanced understanding and right principles are ignored by the modern media. When it comes to issues of civil government and separation of church and state, the Baptists alone have the correct understanding.

*We maintain like John Clarke, Roger Williams, Isaac Backus, John Leland, and Thomas Jefferson that there must be a separation of church and state; however, this does not have to mean a complete removal of Christianity from our federal government!

Baptist Blood, the Purchase Price of Liberty

To this point in the current study we have only mentioned the various ways in which the Puritan theocrats punished our forebears for having the audacity to "obey God rather than men." Now we will highlight an incident of severe proportions. You are about to read a sobering account of religious persecution on American soil. This piece of history, though intentionally hidden from our generation by Satan, had such a profound effect on our yet to be nation that every Baptist ought to know its details.

*The Public Whipping of Obadiah Holmes

Early Life — Obadiah Holmes was born in Reddish, England, near Manchester in the year 1606. He worked on his father's farm as a boy in an England that mostly practiced Puritanism. At this time, England was under the rule of King James I. In his teen years, Holmes saw England returned to rigid Anglicanism as Charles I took the crown. Charles appointed William Laud as bishop of London. Laud then became the Archbishop of Canterbury, or religious head of the Church of England. Laud began to persecute Baptists, Puritans, and other dissidents. He beat and imprisoned many. This activity resulted in many Englishmen, mostly Puritans with some Baptists, sailing for New England in hope of religious liberty. Holmes was one such man. He was married to Catherine Hyde in 1630, accepted Christ in 1638, and sailed that same year to New England.

A Trip to the New World — The Holmes family settled in Salem; but after much conflict with the religionists there, he moved to Seekonk (Massachusetts Bay Colony). It was here that Holmes began to resist the false teaching of the standing order church. He was tormented inside with questions like, *"Was baptism legitimate for infants?"* and, *"What if you were baptized but not a believer?"* Then, amazingly, Obadiah Holmes, with no prior religious training, started a "Separate" Congregational church. This courageous act shook up the "standing order" and Holmes was totally ostracized. Later, in 1649, Dr. Clarke came to town. Under his preaching, Holmes got assurance of his salvation, realized he was a Baptist, and was baptized by Clarke. Before we examine the beating of Obadiah Holmes, we need to realize that he and Dr. John Clarke were marked men by the standing order.

A Trip to Lynn, Massachusetts — In 1651, Obadiah Holmes was found to be a member in good standing at the first Baptist church on American soil, founded and pastored by John Clarke at Newport, Rhode Island. In the summer of 1651, the Newport church received from the aged William Witter a request of visitation, so that he might hear the Word of God. Witter was a man of conviction himself. A strong Baptist, Witter was more than willing to speak out against the state-church and infant, non-Baptist baptism. Here are just a few of the statements Witter made when dragged into court over the issue of baptism:

- "The baptism of infants is sinful."
- "Infant baptism is the badge of the whore."
- "They who stay whiles a child is baptized do worship the devil." (Salem court records, 1644 and 1645)

Witter was a member of the First Baptist Church in Newport, Rhode Island. Being up in years now and blind, he was not able to travel to what was not only the nearest Baptist church, the First Baptist Church, but one of the only organized Baptist churches on American soil. So, upon Witter's request for a pastoral visit, Pastor John Clarke, active layman John Crandall, and preacher Obadiah Holmes started out for Lynn, Massachusetts. After navigating to the mainland and then walking for two days, the men completed the eighty-mile trip. They arrived at Witter's home on Saturday night, July 19, 1651. They enjoyed a time of fellowship and prayer that night while staying at Witter's home, intending to have church services on the Lord's Day. News in Lynn spread fast, and a warrant for the arrest of the strangers was delivered to the constable.

A Trip to the State-Church — Holmes and company began their service the next morning, and after four or five visitors came, the constables burst in to break it up. The three men were taken into custody. The same day, the men were forced to attend an afternoon service in the standing order Congregational church. This Puritan-run state-church was the approved church of the Massachusetts Bay Colony. It is amazing how quickly those who fled religious persecution in England became the persecutors of the Baptists! Upon entering the meeting house, the three bowed and saluted the assembly and sat down, refusing to remove their hats thus showing their contempt for religion. The constable was commanded to knock off their hats, which he did so promptly. Clarke attempted to preach and was silenced. They were then taken to prison.

A Trip to Boston — On Tuesday, July 22, 1651, Holmes, Clarke, and Crandall were taken to Boston, so that they might appear before their adversaries. They were committed to jail and on July 31 they were tried in court. After an animated courtroom frenzy in which Clarke showed what an articulate defender of Baptist doctrine he was, the judge agreed with the prosecutor, Puritan preacher John Cotton, that this heresy (Anabaptism) was worthy of death. There really was no trial, just a reading of the allegations and a commencement with their sentencing. Clarke was fined twenty pounds or be "well whipt," Holmes thirty pounds or be "well whipt," and Crandall five pounds or be "well whipt." Money was raised to pay the fines. Crandall was released from the fine. Clarke and Holmes refused permission for their fines to be paid, not willing to admit guilt, knowing the dreaded whipping post was the alternative.

A Trip to the Dreaded Whipping Post (September 5) — As Clarke was led to the whipping post, a friend pressed money into the hands of the Puritan official accompanying the party, and Clarke was released. But Holmes stated, *"Agreeing to the payment of my fine would constitute admission of wrongdoing."* Holmes was led to the post and stripped to the waist. While being stripped, Obadiah Holmes preached a sermon to the on-looking crowd, exhorting them to stay faithful to their beliefs. Obadiah Holmes' sentence was ten stripes less than the maximum of forty lashes, which was considered a death sentence. Holmes' sentence was the same as that of rapists. Many in the gathering crowd cried out in protest. At least thirteen individuals were arrested for calling for the punishment to stop. The beating was an attempt to kill Holmes. Holmes later stated that the flogger used a whip with three hard leather lashes. The man stopped three times to spit on his hands, and applied the whip with all his might. Each of the thirty strokes cut three gashes through the skin, for a total of ninety slices through the flesh. Holmes gave this account of his beating:

> As the man began to lay the strokes upon my back, I said to the people, though my flesh should fail, yet God will not fail: so it pleased the Lord to come in, and fill my heart and tongue as a vessel full, and with audible voice I break forth, praying the Lord not to lay this sin to their charge, and telling the people I found He did not fail me, and therefore now I should trust Him forever who failed me not: for in truth, as the strokes fell upon me, I had such a spiritual manifestation of God's presence as I never had before and the outward pain was so removed from me, that I could well bear it, yea, and in a manner felt it not, although it was grievous.

The Crack of this Whip Was Heard Across the Land

The unbroken spirit of Holmes and the Baptists of New England was exemplified in the statement Holmes made to the magistrates as he was released from the post. He boldly stated, *"Ye have beaten me as with roses."* This cruel beating did not stop the Baptists; rather it emboldened them.

The Effects of Holmes' Beating:
- John Spur, an on-looker, later testified that being moved powerfully by the faith of Holmes, he was born again at the beating.
- John Spur and John Hazel helped Holmes from the bloody post and were imprisoned. The aged Hazel later died and never returned to Newport, suffering from complications relating to his imprisonment.
- John Clarke, Holmes' pastor, being proficient in law, medicine, and theology, upon the beating of Holmes wrote a book, *Ill Newes from New England* (1652). In it, Dr. Clarke presented his philosophy of government. He pushed for government not to interfere with man's conscience on religious matters.
- Valentine Wightman, on February 10, 1702, married Susannah Holmes, granddaughter to Brother Obadiah Holmes and great-granddaughter of Roger Williams (who was called, "The Apostle of Freedom of Conscience"). Later in 1712, Wightman left Rhode Island, won converts, and started the First Baptist Church of New York City. Holmes has a godly offspring.
- Wightman won Wait Palmer to Christ. Palmer, then pastoring in North Stonington, immersed Shubal Stearns, who became the "Fa-

ther of the Separate Baptists." Shubal Stearns deserves more credit than anyone else for the explosion of the Gospel in the South, which became known as the Bible-belt. Shubal Stearns started the Sandy Creek Baptist Church, which in two generations birthed thousands of churches.
- Henry Dunster, president of Cambridge (now Harvard) University, stirred by Holmes' beating, stood against infant baptism and was forced to resign his position at Cambridge in 1657. Dunster spread Baptist beliefs loudly and influenced Cambridge and neighboring Charlestown until the first Baptist church of Massachusetts Bay Proper was established.
- Thomas Gould, influenced by Dunster, became a warrior for religious freedom. Bulldozing through the courts, his efforts aided in the establishment of the first Baptist church in Boston.

A Trip Back to Newport

After his scourging, Holmes journeyed back to the freedom of Newport. For twenty days and nights, he could sleep only by lying on his stomach or propped upon his knees and elbows. Many sleepless nights reminded him of that day on the Boston square where the blood ran down his back and into his shoes. After Clarke, Holmes pastored the church in Newport.

A Trip Back to Reality

One might ask, "What's the point?" Baptists today sit unmolested, undisturbed, worshipping Jesus Christ, practicing Baptist baptism, tithing to our own churches of our own free will, and preaching with complete liberty granted to us because of courageous acts like the refusal of Holmes and others to admit to the charge that being a Bible-believing Baptist is a sin. Illegal search and seizure laws are on the books today in a big part because the framers of the Constitution took note of what happened at Witter's home and the homes of others throughout the colonial history.

Learning from History
- We and our children owe a great debt of gratitude to our forefathers.
- We owe it to our children to give them these inspiring facts of history.
- We owe it to our God to stand for Him in our generation like Obadiah Holmes and the New England Baptists did!

Review Questions

1. As the baptized believers in New England began to multiply, so did their _____.

2. There were, at times, _____ Christians persecuting _____ Christians.

3. Puritans were simply people who wanted to _____ the Church of _____.

4. Baptists in New England championed the cause for a limited civil _____.

5. John Clarke and Roger Williams believed that the state should not attempt to enforce the _____ _____ of the law.

6. The state's responsibility is to oversee the enforcement of the _____ _____ of the law.

7. The Puritans were _____. Because of this theological error, they believed in _____ theology.

8. Williams spoke of a "_____ of separation." Williams used the analogy of a _____ enclosed for the church.

9. The God of the Bible and our forefathers believed that the church should shed its _____ _____ on the state.

10. Many today believe it is a _____ to declare that there is a separation of church and state.

11. The religious right is running around hollering to all who will listen that there is no such thing as _____ of church and state.

12. The reason the religious right feels this way is because they, like the Puritans, are _____. The religious right is not governed by _____ _____ principles.

13. We maintain like John Clarke, Roger Williams, Isaac Backus, John Leland, and Thomas Jefferson, that there must be a separation of church and state; however, this does not have to mean a complete _____ of Christianity from our _____ _____!

14. Obadiah Holmes, with no prior religious training, started a "Separate" _____ church.

15. Holmes got assurance of his salvation, realized he was a _____, and was baptized by _____.

16. Obadiah Holmes was found to be a _____ in good standing at the first _____ _____ on American soil.

17. Witter stated that infant baptism is the "_____ of the _____."

18. During services in the state run church, the Baptists refused to remove their _____.

19. The judge agreed with John Cotton that Anabaptism was worthy of _____.

20. When released from the post, Obadiah Holmes stated, "____ _____ _____ _____ ____ _____ _____."

Lesson Four

The Great Awakening

…O LORD, revive thy work in the midst of the
years, in the midst of the years make known…
Habakkuk 3:2

One of the greatest revivals in American history was a 1700's outpouring of the Spirit called "The Great Awakening." The Great Awakening began in the mid-1730s and lasted in reasonable strength until the middle part of the 1760s. During these years, untold thousands were converted to the Lord Jesus Christ. Many meetings, some known only to God, experienced multiple conversions during this timeframe.

The Great Awakening began as a two-pronged event. The first great moving of God came in the form of many lost church members being saved in the Congregational state-churches in America. The lightning rod in the midst of this storm was a Standing Order preacher named Jonathan Edwards. Before the Awakening began, the halfway covenant was instituted and heavily practiced in the vast majority of the state-churches. This covenant allowed parents, whether saved or unsaved, to submit their children for infant baptism and subsequent membership in these churches. Because of this, the churches began to fill up with lost people. This, of course, sent the churches into a moral decline very swiftly. The majority of preachers in the establishment churches of New England were mostly orators of dead orthodoxy and not preachers of a heart-felt religion. According to Edwards himself, the Awakening really began in 1734. This was seven years before he preached his famed message, *"Sinners in the Hands of an Angry God."* Based on this timeframe, we conclude that Edwards was not a source of revival, but merely a minister who experienced a stirring himself by God's Holy Spirit. From 1734 to 1741 there were numerous people being awakened who sought the help of Edwards to get their lives right with God. These numbers would multiply over the next several years. During this same time, the geography of the revival would shift. It would grow from Northampton, Massachusetts, spill into nearly every street and home in that state, and then stretch out to almost the whole of New England. While Christians were shaken, lost church members, brought in through the halfway covenant and whose only hope had been baptism, were heartily saved.

The second prong of the Great Awakening began in Old England. England, now in a rapid spiritual decline itself, would produce a minister- the likes of which has rarely been seen in all of history. The minister, who has been referred to by every name of admiration imaginable, such as "Elijah of Old," found himself in the middle of one of the greatest outpourings of the Spirit of God that has ever been evidenced. His name was George Whitefield, and his motto was very simple: "Ye must be born again." As the Lord stirred up the American colonies, He at the same time poured out without measure His Spirit upon the preaching ministry of George Whitefield. Whitefield, like Jonathan Edwards, turned the tide of the status quo and shook up his own denomination (Anglicanism) to the point in which the establishment all but disowned him. His preaching was so contrary to the dead orthodoxy of the Church of England that he stood out like a "light that shineth in a dark place." Whitefield started young and spent the rest of his life preaching the everlasting Gospel. From the time that he preached his first sermon as a young deacon in the Church of England until he preached his final sermon from the stairs of his chamber behind the Newburyport Church, he drew unusually large crowds of people and saw multitudes saved by the grace of God. The life and ministry of this man caused such a change to the spiritual condition of both Europe and America that it is vitally important that every Christian study and understand the powerful ministry of George Whitefield. Matthew Henry stated it this way:

> There are remains of great and good men, which, like Elijah's mantle, ought to be gathered up and preserved by the survivors—their sayings, their writings, their examples; that as their works follow them in the reward of them, they may stay behind in the benefit of them.

It is understandable that the student of Baptist history, at this point, may wonder what this has to do with our Baptist heritage. This is a common and honest question that is often put forth. The answer to this question will be fully laid out, not only during this lesson, but in the following lessons as well. But, for now, let it suffice to say that God both authored and used the Great Awakening. He did this not only for the purpose of those under its immediate influence, but He would use this Awakening to pave the way for a more scriptural and longer lasting revival, called the Separate Baptist Revival. The author is of the firm belief that one cannot understand the greatest revival in American history, the Separate Baptist Revival, until one fully understands the Great Awakening. Armed with this understanding of history, we will now endeavor to present the narrative of the Great Awakening.

Lesson Four

A Land Ripe for Revival

For a Great Awakening to have occurred at all, presupposes that wherever it took place there must have previously existed masses of people in a spiritual slumber. That certainly was the case. We already mentioned that the Great Awakening was a two-pronged event. It began simultaneously in two locales. Because of this fact, it is understandable that these two locales were also in a state of moral decay prior to 1730. The spiritual dearth in these two lands will be briefly examined so as to understand fully the spiritual revival they would experience.

America's Spiritual Stagnation-Halfway Covenant

> In the opening years of the 1700s the halfway covenant gained much approval and had a chilling effect on the churches of the Standing Order. The baptism of infant children was the common practice under this corrupt system. Unsaved parents, who were not members and were unqualified for communion themselves, began to bring their children to partake of this evil act. From the very beginning of colonial life, the colonies struggled with this practice. The standing order churches, with the exception of those in Connecticut, were mostly resistant to the halfway covenant.
>
> The Baptists preached publicly against this practice and were punished for doing so. The Baptist

sentiment in colonial America is best expressed by William Witter. He was the man in whose home Obadiah Holmes was arrested. Witter stated, *"The baptism of infants is sinful"* and *"They who stay whiles a child is baptized do worship the devil."* He further stated that infant baptism is *"the badge of the whore"* (Salem court records 1644 and 1645). This was the common sentiment held by Baptists towards the halfway covenant and infant baptism. This horrible error destroyed the Biblical doctrine of the new birth through personal faith in Christ. Jonathan Edwards found himself in the midst of a controversy of his own at this time. His grandfather, on his mother's side was Solomon Stoddard. Stoddard was a respected, Standing Order preacher and a leading proponent of the halfway covenant. Though difficult to do, Edwards, in spite of his great respect for his grandfather, chose the side of truth on this issue. He saw its error as is evidenced by the following statement: Baptism in the Standing Order churches was "viewed as a converting ordinance."

(*Memoirs of Jonathan Edwards* by Sorano E. Dwight)

Although the Baptists in America wholeheartedly rejected the halfway covenant, as much as they did the whole of Puritan congregationalism, they were having some spiritual problems themselves. Sadly, Calvinism was growing more popular. The Regular or Particular Baptists perpetuated the teachings of particular redemption, otherwise known as Calvinism. In addition to this, there was a general laxness creeping in to Baptist assemblies of all stripes.

Historian John Comer summed up the condition among the Baptists in his diary. In February of 1730, he wrote the following: "The interest of Christ in the Baptist churches looks very dark at this time; the harvest is great, but the labourers are few. Oh that the Lord of the harvest would furnish and send forth into His harvest! I mourn over the churches. Lord show us, what is the ground of thy controversie?"

Slow Growth Before the Great Awakening

All one has to do to discover evidence of America's spiritual need prior to 1730 is to simply compare the numbers of churches that came into existence in the first century of Baptist labor with the number of churches that were birthed within the next half century. Before the Great Awakening started, there were very few sparks of revival to be seen. We are thankful for the hard fought ground that was gained in New England among the Baptists. We also recognize the labor of the churches in the Philadelphia Association (founded in 1707). The truth is, however, that the greatest work among the Baptists was still futuristic. We do not recognize the Great Awakening itself as a strictly Baptist revival, or even a mostly Baptist revival. We do want to point out, however, that at the time of the Awakening, a revival among the Baptists would begin and grow to wonderful proportions.

Jehovah Visits America With A Time of Great Harvest
Jonathan Edwards

The Great Awakening began in the early 1730s. Jonathan Edwards was a Standing Order, Congregational pastor. God lit a fire under him and he experienced an anointing of Holy Spirit power upon his preaching. His powerful preaching introduced revival to his Northampton, Massachusetts church in 1734. He preached on the subject of the new birth. He preached zealously to the end that men might surrender completely to the Holy Spirit in their lives. He knew well of surrender. His preaching had much influence among the people, not only because of the Holy Ghost anointing on the Word of God, but also because he lived what he preached. He was a man of self denial. He knew what it was to beat down his body and bring it into subjection. He, like Whitefield, fasted often, spent long seasons in prayer, and missed much sleep. In 1741 he preached his most powerful sermon "Sinners in the Hands of an Angry God," at the Parish Church of Enfield, Connecticut. By 1736 at least twenty different churches of the standing order were experiencing a host of conversions as well as a moving of the Holy Ghost in their services. Between the years of 1737 and 1740 the revival began to taper off significantly. Soon, however, the flames would be fanned by the whirlwind from England, George Whitefield.

George Whitefield

The second wave of revival was ignited by God through an Anglican preacher named George Whitefield.

Early Life

George Whitefield was born in Gloucester, England on December 16, 1714, the sixth son born to Elizabeth Whitefield. His father would pass on when he was two years old. Although his mother wished for him to have spiritual inclinations, he was an average, irreverent, worldly, English lad. He, according to his own testimony, loved to steal money from his mother, play cards, watch plays and romances, and play tricks on people. He called such worldly things "my heart's delight." He evidenced early in his teen years a good memory and much talent in delivering speeches and play acting. Some have wrongly stated that these natural abilities shaped his future preaching ministries. Whitefield himself tells quite another story. He believed that in the performance of plays he learned carnality, not oratory ability. He stated:

I got acquainted with such a set of debauched, abandoned, atheistical youths that if God, by his free, unmerited, and special grace, had not delivered me out of their hands, I should have sat in the scorner's chair, and made a mock at sin. By keeping company with them, my thoughts of religion grew more and more like theirs. I went to public service only to make sport, and walk about. I took pleasure in their lewd conversation. I began to reason as they did, and to ask why God had given me passions, and not permitted me to gratify them. In short, I soon made great proficiency in the school of the devil. I affected to look rakish, and was in a fair way of being as infamous as the worst of them.

(Joseph Belcher, *Biography of Whitefield*, p. 27)

Strange Drawing to the Ministry

Whitefield left off schooling at fifteen years of age and proceeded to help his mother tend the family business. He worked at the inn with his blue apron donned, washing mops and cleaning rooms. At this time the Lord inclined unto him and began a work in his heart. A desire to be a minister was placed on him from the Lord. Still unconverted, Whitefield fits the pattern of the author as well as countless other ministers through the ages, who, as lost children, felt a tug at the heart toward being a preacher. Whitefield said, "[I] was always fond of being a clergyman, and used frequently to imitate the ministers' reading prayers." He began to read the Bible late at night. He also wrote sermons and preached them to his brother.

Oxford Bound

Through a quickly carried out chain of events, George Whitefield was on his way to the Pembroke College in Oxford. He was eighteen years old and his life was about to change forever.

Salvation Found

When he arrived at college, he was much dismayed at the sad, spiritual condition of the students there. Deadness and orthodoxy were the law, and non-conformists were still very unacceptable. He became withdrawn and spent much time alone in his room. God knew what He was doing in directing this poor, lost soul to Oxford for here is where Mr. Whitefield would meet the men that would direct him to true salvation. The men were the famous Wesley brothers, John and Charles. Whitefield joined the "Holy Club" and began to seek God. After much pain and self denial, Whitefield found freedom in his soul and was converted.

John 4: The Woman at the Well

According to his own testimony, Whitefield became much like the woman at the well. He was consumed in telling others to "Come, see a man" (Jesus Christ). He wrote:

> Upon this, like the woman of Samaria, when Christ revealed himself to her at the well I had no rest in my soul till I wrote letters to my relation, telling them there was such a thing as the new birth. I imagined they would have gladly received it; but, alas, my words seemed to them as idle tales. They thought I was going beside myself.
>
> (Joseph Belcher, *Biography of George Whitefield*, p. 34)

He not only attempted to evangelize his relations, he also went to a local jail daily to read and pray to those there. He witnessed to the poor several times a week and attended church regularly.

His Ordination and First Sermon

Whitefield begged God on several occasions not to send him until he felt ready to preach. He believed he was "unfit to preach in [His] great name." But the bishop kept pleading with him to go into orders before his twenty-second birthday. Finally he surrendered to the Lord. He was ordained on Sunday, June 20, 1736, in the cathedral in Gloucester. This newly ordained deacon in the Church of England wasted no time in carrying out his duties. His first sermon was preached on the very next Sunday. Later, it was revealed that he drove fifteen people mad when he preached. When he first preached in London, he recorded at least one shout of "boy parson." Soon, however, the whole world would know that this was not a "boy parson" but a "holy man of God."

Whitefield Comes to America

In 1735 the Wesley brothers embarked for Georgia in America. They were in a search for souls. John and Charles Wesley were much interested in fanning the flames of revival in America. To this end they pressed. Charles journeyed back to London, England, and petitioned Whitefield with much pleading to come to America. Finally he complied. His arrival was in 1739. His subsequent tour of the middle and southern colonies was very successful and greatly received. He returned to England later that year but would return to America in August of 1739. This time the fire of God would fall tremendously.

Cry Aloud, Spare Not

When I think of the preaching of Whitefield, a Scripture comes to mind. Isaiah 58:1 reads, "Cry aloud, spare not, lift up thy voice like a trumpet and shew my people their transgression, and the house of Jacob their sins." Here God told Isaiah what the people needed. This must have been what the Lord did with Whitefield. Just as Israel was in a state of spiritual decline, so was America. When this modern-day "prophet of God" preached, it was with several identifiable characteristics.

(A) *Biblical*: All authorities on Whitefield agree that the overruling theme and often the only point of his preaching was, "Ye must be born again."

(B) *Anointed*: Just one example of many that could be given is this telling quote from his journal. He said, concerning the Boston meetings, that "many wept exceedingly and cried out under the Word, like persons that were hungering and thirsting after righteousness. The Spirit of the Lord was upon them all."

(C) *Pointed and Loud*: Benjamin Franklin said that Whitefield's sermons could be heard clearly from a mile away.

(D) *Animated*: Whitefield was known to have had an unusual way of painting word pictures. In one instance, he was preaching about the soul of man tossed on life's troubled sea ready to sink at any moment; when in the midst of his preaching, an old seaman of many years stood to his feet and declared with a loud voice, "To the life boats men, to the life boats," thinking himself to be sinking!

Lesson Four

George Whitefield Preaching

Philadelphia

On his second tour, Whitefield preached for nine days in Philadelphia. There was such a move of God and such a number of conversions that the whole city was in an uproar. Those awakened loved him, but the yet spiritually dead clergy wanted his neck!

New York

He rode on horseback to New York and was forced by the Anglican Church to preach in open fields.

New England

Boston was greatly affected. In Northampton, Jonathan Edwards said that his congregation was "melted by every sermon."

Connecticut

It is hard to imagine the labor Whitefield performed. In one instance, he preached over 175 times in 75 consecutive days, place to place. His stops in Connecticut included Suffield, Middleton, East Windsor, Weathersfield, Westfield, Springfield, Hartford, New Haven, Millford, Stratford, Fairfield, Newark, and Stanford. At least six towns saw great revival come to the churches and townspeople. Lumpkin stated that, *"In a brief six-week period, the religious climate of New England was changed."*

As you can imagine, many religious groups felt the effects of the Great Awakening. The Baptists at this time were no exception. Churches were being stirred and new ones planted. Since many people were saved and subsequently studied their Bibles, many of Whitefield's converts became Baptists, much to his dismay. Such a large number of those saved during the Great Awakening joined the Baptists that Whitefield stated, "All my chickens have turned to ducks!"

Lesson Four

Summary

His Death

George Whitefield passed from this life in September of 1770. His remains are buried under the pulpit of the Old South Church (Presbyterian) in Newburyport, Massachusetts.

The Prophet's Mantle Falls on a Baptist

It is said that Whitefield was the most traveled preacher of the Gospel in history up to his timeframe. He preached to untold millions and to over 100,000 people at one time. He crossed the Atlantic Ocean six times to preach. He preached in nearly a dozen countries and had great success everywhere, except for one place- North Carolina.

> In December of 1739, after Whitefield attempted to bring revival to North Carolina and seemingly failed, he wrote the following entry in his journal: "Oh God that thou would send forth a John the Baptist to preach and baptize in the wilderness."
>
> (*Journal entry*, December 26, 1739)

Six years later, as Whitefield preached, a young man named Shubal Stearns was born again. God used the preaching of Whitefield to answer his own prayer request.

Elijah's mantle fell on Elisha, and with that mantle, a double portion. You probably already assumed that the use of Elijah in this analogy is a reference to Whitefield, but who is Elisha? A man called Shubal.

Review Questions

1. One of the greatest revivals in American history was a 1700s outpouring of the Spirit called "The Great _____."

2. The first great moving of God came in the form of many lost church members being saved in the _____ state-churches in America.

3. The _____ covenant allowed parents, whether saved or unsaved, to submit their children for infant baptism.

4. The first prong of the Awakening began in New England and the second began in _____ _____.

5. The author is of the firm belief that one cannot understand the greatest revival in American history, the _____ _____ Revival, until one fully understands the _____ Awakening.

6. Jonathan _____ grandfather, on his mother's side, was Solomon Stoddard.

7. Stoddard was a respected, standing order preacher and a leading proponent of the _____ _____.

8. The Regular or Particular _____ perpetuated the teachings of particular redemption, otherwise known as _____.

9. John Comer wrote: "I mourn over the churches. Lord show us, what is the ground of thy _____?"

10. Jonathan Edwards fasted _____, spent long seasons in _____, and missed much _____.

11. In 1741 Edwards preached his most powerful sermon "_____ _____ _____ _____ _____ ____ _____ _____," at the Parish Church of Enfield, Connecticut.

12. The second wave of revival was ignited by God through an Anglican preacher named _____ _____.

13. Whitefield was an average, irreverent, worldly, _____ _____.

14. He began to read the _____ much late at night. He also wrote sermons and preached them to his _____.

15. George Whitefield attended the _____ College in _____.

16. At college, Whitefield met _____ and _____ Wesley.

17. According to his own testimony, Whitefield became much like the _____ at the _____.

18. Whitefield drove fifteen people _____ when he preached his first sermon.

19. It is true that the preaching of Whitefield was _____.

20. All authorities on Whitefield agree that the overruling theme and often the only point of his preaching was, "Ye _____ _____ _____ _____."

21. Benjamin _____ said that Whitefield's sermons could be heard clearly from a _____ away.

22. In one instance, he preached over _____ times in 75 consecutive days, place to place.

23. Such a large number of those saved during the Great Awakening joined the Baptists that Whitefield stated, "All my _____ have turned to _____!"

24. Whitefield crossed the Atlantic Ocean _____ times to preach. He preached in nearly a _____ countries and had great success everywhere, except for one place - _____ _____.

25. "Oh God that thou would send forth a _____ _____ _____ to preach and baptize in the wilderness."

Lesson Five

Shubal Stearns and the Separate Baptists

> Oh that thou wouldest rend the heavens, that thou wouldest come down, that the mountains might flow down at thy presence.
>
> **Isaiah 64:1**

As one examines the Great Awakening and its overall effects on our nation, it is inevitable that the attention must quickly turn to the South. Of all areas under the immediate power of Whitefield and the Awakening, it is agreed that the South saw the least revival and the lowest numbers of converts. New churches multiplied in the North at a much faster pace, and Whitefield himself admitted his frustration concerning the overall disinterest in the things of God in the South and specifically in North Carolina. That being said, it would be the South, and North Carolina in particular, where the breath of God would blow on the souls of men, much like it did on Pentecost. Dr. James Beller stated it this way:

> History is buried at Sandy Creek, beneath endless winter, summer heat, and the leaves of two centu-

ries of autumn. We thank our Heavenly Father that such history can be resurrected, for there on those sleepy hillsides the settlers witnessed quite possibly, **the greatest outpouring of the Holy Ghost on a group of believers since the day of Pentecost.**

(Dr. James Beller, *America in Crimson Red,* pg. 144)

The Sandy Creek area in North Carolina was the place, and Shubal Stearns was the man that stood at the southern crossroads of a nation and the crossroads of history. This man, by simply choosing to serve God with all of his heart, found himself in the center of a Holy Ghost blizzard of blessings. To simply say God showed up is the equivalent of saying the Titanic had a bad day or Custer didn't necessarily win at Little Bighorn. Reader, prepare yourself to read a piece of history that is so vital to our generation that the devil has tried with all his power to conceal it from Baptists today. You will not understand the Great Awakening until you understand Sandy Creek, Stearns, and the Separate Baptist Revival. You will not understand America, and what shaped it, until you understand the lesson you are about to study. You may not understand fully what needs to be done today to reclaim America for God until you are acquainted with the Separate Baptist Revival. In recent years, men have unearthed the jewels you are about to put under the microscope;

these men have never been the same. The history of Sandy Creek has excited, stirred, caused men to weep, and moved untold numbers of Baptists today to plant churches, win souls, and dig deeper into their heritage in hopes that they just might strike another golden vein of Baptist history.

America was already in an Awakening. What was about to happen in North Carolina was the spiritual pinnacle of all religious activity in American history!

Giants in the Land

Shubal Stearns was born in Boston on the 28th of January in the year 1706. His parents, Shubal and Rebecca, moved the family to Tolland, Connecticut. Although he was a member of the Congregational church for a time, his doctrinal position changed in the same year his spiritual position changed. He was saved under the preaching of George Whitefield and accepted Whitefield's doctrinal views concerning the deadness and error in the state churches.

A New Light Pastor

Stearns removed from the Congregational church with a group of others awakened to its error, and together they formed a New Light church. Stearns was their pastor. During this timeframe, Stearns came into contact with a Baptist preacher from North Stonington named Wait Palmer. After hearing Palmer preach on an itinerant tour, Stearns took up the issue of scriptural baptism and did not put it down until he settled it in his heart. When the dust cleared, he knew he was a Baptist. Upon his scriptural discovery, he submitted to be scripturally baptized by Palmer in 1751.

A Baptist Pastor

Upon Stearns sharing his views with the members of his church, many of them withdrew from all forms of Congregationalism, and the group formed a Baptist church in Tolland. Stearns was both ordained and installed as the pastor of this new Baptist assembly on the same day. The date was May 20, 1751, and the ordination committee was composed of Pastor Wait Palmer and Pastor Joshua Morse, the pastor in Monville, Connecticut.

A Baptist Missionary

By 1754, Stearns was discontented with the ministry in Tolland. He, like many others who had left before him, believed that there was a great harvest of souls to be had for the taking. His sister, Martha Stearns Marshall, and brother-in-law, Daniel, had left a few years prior in search of Indian souls. A burden from God could not be shaken; and so in August of 1754, a party of roughly a dozen Baptists left Tolland. They made stops in New York and Philadelphia. This group, with cart in tow, eventually ended up in Hampshire County, Virginia.

At this point, Daniel Marshall and Stearns' sister met the group and joined in the survey and work in this area. They built simple dwellings and quickly took up residence. Stearns began to fervently preach in this area, but this would not be his final stop. Isaac Backus records for us that Stearns received a letter from North Carolina. Stearns alludes to the letter in one that he wrote and sent to Connecticut. While he was still in southern Virginia, Stearns wrote, "that the work of God was great in preaching to an ignorant people, who had little or no preaching for a hundred miles, and no established meeting. But now the people were so eager to hear, that they would come forty miles each way, when they could have opportunity to hear a sermon" (William Lumpkin, *Baptist Foundations in the South,* pg. 29). With this need at heart, the group left for North Carolina.

Beautiful for Situation

In Psalm 48:2, God states that the land He put the Jews in was in the perfect place, "beautiful for situation," He calls it. This is partly because they were in somewhat of a crossroad area and would therefore be able to be a good testimony to many lost people coming through. In like manner, it appears very obvious that God directed Stearns and Marshall to the Sandy Creek area. Again, Dr. James Beller in his *America in Crimson Red* explains:

> In 1755, three forest paths traversed the province of North Carolina. The Settlers Road, also known as the Great Wagon Road, ran from north to south all the way from Pennsylvania to South Carolina.

Depiction of the First Service of the Sandy Creek Baptist Church

(Artist rendering, commissioned by the Baptist History Preservation Society)

Secondly, what eventually became known as the Boone Trail, ran west from Wilmington to the Yadkin settlements. Thirdly, the Trading Path, came from southeastern Virginia (Norfolk) to the Waxhaw country.

> Those three trails converged on a little notch in the wilderness of North Carolina by the waters of Sandy Creek. That spot, which is nearly remote today, was in the days of the Separate Baptist Revival a national crossroads between north and south (pp. 142-143).

It is good to remember that this field was ripe. Up to this time in history, there were less than twenty-five total churches in Virginia, North Carolina, and South Carolina combined. Georgia had none and Tennessee was still more than a decade from their first church. Of those that existed in the South before the arrival of the Separates, most were somewhat dead and/or Calvinistic. The two groups already there were the General and Particular Baptists.

The Church Established

Semple records, "As soon as they arrived, they built them a simple meeting house." They began with sixteen members and chose Stearns as their pastor. Joseph Breed and Daniel Marshall were his assistants.

A Unique Church
Unusual Preaching

The preaching of Shubal Stearns must have been a real treat in which to partake. The testimony of God's power on this man's pulpit ministry has been preserved for us. Lumpkin called Stearns a "matchless preacher" and stated that the initial hearers "could not decide which was more remarkable the content or the delivery."

William Cathcart said of Stearns, "He was eloquent, wise, humble, pathetic, full of faith, and wholly consecrated to God, and few men ever enjoyed more of the Spirit's presence in the closet and in preaching the gospel. He was undoubtedly one of the greatest ministers that ever presented Jesus to perishing multitudes, and one of the most successful soul-winners that ever unfurled the banner of Calvary."

Tidence Lane described his conversion under Stearns' preaching this way:

> When the fame of Mr. Stearns' preaching reached the Yadkin where I lived, I felt a curiosity to go and hear him. Upon my arrival I saw a venerable man sitting under a peach-tree with a book in his hand and the people gathering about him. He fixed his eyes upon me immediately, which made me feel in such a manner as I had never felt before. I turned to quit the place, but could not proceed far. I walked about, sometimes catching his eyes as I walked. My uneasiness increased and became intolerable. I went up to him, thinking that a salutation and shaking of hands would relieve me; but it happened otherwise. I began to think he had an evil eye and ought to be shunned, but shunning him I could no more effect

than a bird can shun the rattlesnake when it fixes its eyes upon it. When he began to preach my perturbations increased so that nature could no longer support them and I sank to the ground.

Elnathan Davis went to hear Stearns one night with a group of rowdies but was so gripped, that after some time, he trembled and sank to the ground. Soon after, he was converted.

All of Stearns' preacher boys copied his style and zeal. They were loud, pointed, Holy Ghost filled preachers of the Gospel.

Unusual Worship

As strange as this preaching seemed to many, the congregation's response to it was equally troubling. The Particular (Calvinistic) Baptists viewed the excitement and noisy worship style of the Separate Baptists as "disorderly" and excessive. Regularly the church people testified as people wept, cried out, shouted and rejoiced. They were interested in letting the Holy Spirit have total control to cause men to freely worship. Morgan Edwards pointed out that "crying out under the ministry" of Stearns was quite normal for the Separate Baptists.

Unbelievable Growth

The growth of the Separate Baptists in the South

was truly an amazing work. Sandy Creek Church grew from sixteen to over six hundred in two years. Then Sandy Creek began to raise up and send out ministers with unprecedented speed. This tree had spread its branches far and wide at a rate for which only God could be responsible.

David Benedict commenting on their growth said:

> Sandy Creek Church is the mother of all the Separate Baptists. From this Sion went forth the word, and great was the company of them who published it, insomuch that her converts were as drops of morning dew. This church in seventeen years has spread her branches westward as far as the great river Mississippi; southward as far as Georgia; eastward to the sea and Chesapeake Bay; and northward to the waters of the Potomac; it, in seventeen years, is become mother, grandmother, and great-grandmother, to forty-two churches, from which sprang 125 ministers.

The Separate Baptists are almost wholly responsible for the saturation of the South with the Gospel and local churches. Dr. David Cummins stated, *"The Bible Belt should be renamed the Separate Baptist Belt."* One hundred twenty-five preachers sprang from the first twenty-one churches.

Churches started directly out of Sandy Creek are as follows:

Sandy Creek, 1755
1. Abbots Creek, 1756
2. Grassy Creek, 1756
3. Deep River, 1757
4. New River, 1758
5. Little River, 1759
6. Dan River, 1759
7. Black River, 1760
8. Fairforest, 1760
9. Trent, 1761
10. Southwest, 1762
11. Haw River, 1764
12. Congaree, 1766
13. Stephen's Creek, 1766
14. Upper Spottsylvania, 1767
15. Staughton River, 1768
16. Shallow Fords, 1768
17. Lower Spottsylvania, 1769
18. Fall Creek, 1769
19. Goochland, 1771
20. Lockwood's Folly, 1772

In addition to these first generation church plants, Little River started four churches by 1769. They are as follows: Little River 2, Rocky River, Jones Creek, and Mountain Creek.

Haw River also birthed five churches in 1772:

Deep River 2, Rocky River 2, Tick Creek, Collins Mount, and Caraway Creek.

That makes a total of at least thirty churches planted by the Separate Baptists in the first seventeen years.

First Churches

Tennessee would get its first Baptist church—Buffalo Ridge. This church founded in late 1778 was started by Tidence Lane, who was saved under Stearns.

Georgia—Daniel Marshall founded, with much persecution, the Kiokee Baptist Church in 1772. His ministry was phenomenal. He personally gathered at least thirteen churches that we know of in at least four states. He personally gathered the first Separate Baptist church in Virginia of which Dutton Lane took the helm.

Sandy Creek Association

Along with the church, Stearns founded the Sandy Creek Association for the purpose of encouraging the brethren. The first meeting was in June of 1758. There on the grounds of Sandy Creek Baptist Church, the American camp meeting was born. Most meetings were mainly comprised of preaching, testifying, and sharing "good news from a far land." Large crowds gathered in October of each

Lesson Five

year for this meeting. Preacher boys would travel in. The air was filled with rejoicing.

James Reed gave the following report of the first meeting:

> At our first Association we continued together three or four days; great crowds of people attended, mostly through curiosity. The great power of God was among us; the preaching every day seemed to be attended with God's blessing. We carried on our Association with sweet decorum and fellowship to the end. Then we took our leave of one another with many solemn charges from our reverend old father, Shubal Stearns, to stand fast unto the end (William Lumpkin, *Baptist Foundations in the South*, pg. 46).

In 1770 the Sandy Creek Association divided into three parts. Sandy Creek continued to be the association for North Carolina. South Carolina called its association Congaree and the Virginia Separate Baptists named their group the General Association of the Separate Baptists of Virginia. This solved the problem of traveling to the annual meeting as well as the other minor differences that arose.

This was the greatest revival in American history!
It was Biblical

This revival, unlike the Great Awakening, was

local church based. It was also not just open air preaching, but involved organizing converts, administering baptism, and planting local churches with permanence as a focus. Stearns' ministry was much more similar to the apostle Paul's then the Anglican Whitefield's ever was.

It was Long Lasting

Because of the belief of Baptists that the Biblical pattern is churches starting churches, some have stated that every time a scriptural church is birthed in America, the Separate Baptist Revival continues. Knowing the true scope of this revival, it is difficult for the author to imagine that there are many Baptist churches in existence today that are in no way attached or influenced in some way by this mighty move of God.

It was Far Reaching

This revival gave several regions and states their first, truly scriptural churches. The entire South was not just awakened, but much of it was saved by the grace of God.

Many believe that by 1825 well over 2,000 churches were birthed as a direct result of Stearns and the Separate Baptist Revival.

The "Reverend Old Father" Departs This Life

On November 20, 1771, "Reverend Old Father," Shubal Stearns died amid his labors at the age of sixty-five. His sixteen-year mission to the South was completed. He was the chief light and the guiding genius behind the Separate Baptist movement. There can be no doubt that he planted well, for forty-two churches and one hundred and twenty-five ministers had sprung from the Sandy Creek Church by 1772. The Baptist movement had been securely planted from the Potomac River southward into Georgia, and from the Atlantic westward to the mountains. Rarely has a religious leader seen such rapid and magnificent results from a few years of labor. Surely the Lord was in it. It should be marked, however, that in North Carolina itself Separate Baptist churches were not actually so numerous in 1771. There were many branches of the existing churches, but emigration had taken a heavy toll on church life. Some of the oldest and strongest churches had been dissolved for this reason. Even Sandy Creek was greatly decimated by 1772. [Other reasons for this will be discussed shortly.] Stearns lived only long enough to see foundations laid in North Carolina and beyond; he saw fires started here and there which would not be quenched. In the confidence that God's fires cannot be put out, he fell asleep.

(William Lumpkin, *Baptist Foundations in the South*, pg. 59)

Review Questions

1. The Separate Baptist Revival has been referred to by Dr. Beller as possibly the "greatest outpouring of the _____ _____ on a group of believers since the day of _____."

2. The _____ Creek area in North Carolina was the place, and _____ _____ was the man.

3. The Separate Baptist Revival is a piece of history that is so vital to our generation that the _____ has tried with all his power to conceal it from _____ today.

4. You will not understand _____, and what shaped it, until you understand the Separate Baptist Revival.

5. The history of Sandy _____ has excited, stirred, caused men to _____, and moved untold numbers of Baptists today to plant _____.

6. Shubal Stearns was born in _____ on the 28th of January in the year _____.

7. Stearns was saved under the preaching of
_____ _____.

8. Stearns removed from the Congregational _____ with a group of others awakened to its error, and together they formed a _____ _____ church.

9. Stearns was baptized by _____ _____.

10. Stearns started a Baptist church in _____, Connecticut.

11. Stearns was ordained by _____ _____ _____ and _____ _____ _____.

12. Before Stearns settled in North Carolina, he stopped and preached in _____ _____, _____ where he was joined by Marshall.

13. Semple records, "As soon as they arrived, they built them a _____ _____ house."

14. Stearns was "…one of the greatest ministers

that ever presented Jesus to perishing multitudes, and one of the most successful _____-_____ that ever unfurled the _____ of Calvary."

15. Tidence _____ and Elnathan _____ both sank to the ground under his preaching, and both became great Baptist preachers.

16. Regularly the church people testified as people wept, cried out, _____ and _____.

17. Sandy Creek Church grew from _____ to over _____ _____ in two years.

18. Dr. David Cummins stated, "The _____ _____ should be renamed the _____ _____ _____."

19. There were a total of at least _____ churches planted by the Separate Baptists in the first _____ years.

20. Tennessee and_____ both received their first Baptist churches during this time.

21. James Reed related this record of the first associational meeting: "…we took our leave of one another with many solemn charges from our _____ old _____, Shubal Stearns, to stand fast unto the end."

22. Stearns' ministry was much more similar to the _____ Paul's then the _____ Whitefield's ever was.

23. Many believe that by 1825 well over _____ churches were birthed as a direct result of Stearns and the Separate Baptist Revival.

24. Stearns died at the age of _____.

25. Lumpkin said of Stearns, "In the confidence that God's fires _____ be put out, he fell asleep."

Lesson Six

Baptists and the American Revolution

> Then said He unto them...he that hath no sword, let him sell his garment and buy one.
> **Luke 22:36**

By the mid 1760s the Separate Baptist Revival was in full swing. This was a mighty work of God that was gathering steam every year it occurred. The Separate Baptists were being used of God to sew the spiritual fabric of a nation that would for many years experience great blessings from the mighty hand of the Lord.

But at the same time true religion was flourishing, something was brewing in North Carolina. Unforeseen by many Baptists at this time, the American Revolution was just around the next bend.

The influence of the Revolution on the colonies is fairly well known and is a common narrative in American history books. The influence of the Revolution on the Baptists is much less known today, but is fairly noted among informed Baptists of our day. However, the influence of the Baptists on the Revolution and on its victorious outcome is almost completely unknown by Baptists and non-Baptists alike.

In this lesson, we will examine the three previously mentioned areas of study. We will begin to see the Baptists, already greatly responsible for America's spiritual revival, become a religious body that had great influence on America militarily.

The author has often stated that if you take the Separate Baptists out of the picture, the America of today would be a different place spiritually. We owe them a great debt of gratitude. Furthermore, if you take the Baptists out of the picture with their spiritual and military influence on the Revolution deleted, there may not be a United States of America today!

Baptist historian William Cathcart may have said it best in the preface of *Baptist Patriots and the American Revolution:*

> Baptists have ever been the ardent friends of civil and religious liberty. Their history in the New World overflows with testimonies of this character.
>
> They have never regarded the military profession with much favor and, as a rule, have only resorted to arms in great emergencies when the worst evils threatened an entire people. So that we must not look for them among the principal commanders of the Revolution.

> The leading men of Massachusetts and Virginia, the two great arms of the Revolution, were hostile to the Baptists, and had lent their aid to laws which grievously persecuted them right down to the commencement of the great struggle, and it is not to be expected that they would place members of the "Sect everywhere spoken against" in prominent military positions...
>
> Notwithstanding these considerations our brethren acted a glorious part in the conflict, which secured our liberties, and which set the world an example which so many nations have already followed.

Prelude to the Revolution

The American Revolutionary War was not brought on in a day. The fires of revolution were slowly kindled throughout the colonies.

Sugar Act

As early as 1764, public outrage at the British Parliament's tax policy was expressed in North Carolina. On October 31, of this same year, outrage over the Sugar Act was proclaimed as North Carolina legislators denounced the new tax policy.

Stamp Act

In March of 1765, Parliament passed the infamous Stamp Act. Under this act, bills of lading, legal documents, pamphlets, newspapers, and numerous other items were required to carry stamps. On October 19, 1765, over five hundred people in the lower Cape Fear area of North Carolina converged near Wilmington. They demonstrated with a bonfire and mock hanging of Lord Bute. Some historians believe that the "Sons of Liberty" were born on this night. The Sons of Liberty would become a zealous group of patriots who opposed the king and Parliament's taxes and encroachment.

Townshend Act

Parliament passed the Townsend Act in 1767. Duties were placed on imported wine, paper, lead, glass, and tea. On November 11, 1768, the General Assembly of North Carolina offered an address to the king. Speaker of the House John Harvey said, "Free men cannot legally be taxed but by themselves or their representative…" (*A Chronicle of North Carolina during the American Revolution*, p. 9).

On November 2, 1769 Speaker Harvey presented the Virginia resolutions of non-importation to the North Carolina legislature. When the lower house adopted these resolutions, the governor dissolved the assembly. This would prove to be the straw that would break the camel's back.

Lesson Six

Governor Tryon, an Enemy

William Tryon became governor in North Carolina in May of 1765. From the beginning of his governorship, he proved to be an enemy of liberty, self rule, and the Baptist people. Tryon had a corrupt group of subordinates under his leadership. Lumpkin said of Tryon's crew of corrupt politicians that they "pocketed over half of the tax money they collected." He went on to say that the "officials scorned the poor and took advantage of the ignorant."

The provincial assembly was controlled by planters from the East. Tryon lived in the East. Thus, the average North Carolinian was misrepresented or not represented at all.

Governor Tryon Hated Baptists

In 1766 Tryon passed a marriage act that put Baptists and other dissenters on the wrong side of the law if they performed weddings. According to the historian Paschal, Tryon called the Baptists "enemies to society and a scandal to common sense."

The Regulators

As a result of all the corruption, the mistreatment of the Baptists and other dissenting groups, lack of representation, and exorbitant taxes, the Baptists would make history by leading in a liberty movement. These liberty lovers would be called the

Regulation.

The Regulators were largely Baptist groups that stepped to the forefront in opposing Governor Tryon and his corrupt and oppressive government. Benjamin Merrill was a key leader of this movement. Captain Merrill was a member of the Jersey Settlement Baptist Church where John Gano pastored.

The Battle of Alamance

On May 16, 1771, Governor Tryon and his army met the Regulators on a piece of ground near Alamance Creek. In less than two hours, Tryon's force decimated the Regulators. This defeat quenched the immediate fire. But as the sparks flew upward, these sparks would become a great, unquenchable flame called the Revolution.

The Effects of the Battle of Alamance and Governor Tryon on the Baptists of North Carolina

Captain Merrill and five others hanged in Hillsborough

South of Lexington, not far from the Jersey Baptist Church, Benjamin Merrill's plantation was overrun and he was arrested. Chief Justice Howard pronounced the following sentence:

Lesson Six

> "...that you, Benjamin Merrill, be carried to the place from whence you came; that you be drawn from thence to the place of execution, where you are to be hanged by the neck; that you be cut down while yet alive; that your bowels be taken out while you are yet alive and burnt before your face; that your head be cut off, and your body divided into four quarters, and this to be at his Majesty's disposal; and the Lord have mercy on your soul."

(Garland A. Hendricks, *Saints and Sinners*, p. 22)

The North Carolina Baptists Decimated and Driven Away

Tryon and his militia knew the Regulators were mostly Baptists, so he attacked and drove away the Baptists at Sandy Creek, Abbotts Creek, Shallow Fords, Deep Creek, Belew's Creek, Hunting Creek, and Jersey Settlement. He wasted their plantations and apprehended many, putting them in prison.

On page eighty three of *Baptist Foundations in the South*, we read the following:

> "The Sandy Creek folk, nevertheless, knew a week of terror during the encampment of the army, whose intentions could only be guessed. The week was sufficient to convince most members of Sandy Creek Church that they must migrate."

Although Sandy Creek was reduced to less than twenty members at this time, the churches and ministers that she produced would not be stopped. At this time the greatest area of Separate Baptist Revival activity would become Virginia.

The Baptist Regulators Paved the Way for the American Revolution

Garland A. Hendricks stated in his book *Saints and Sinners*, "The kind of defeat which they suffered most certainly made some of the survivors more determined than ever to stand firm upon the principles of freedom and of separation of church and state." The truth of the previous quote would be evidenced in Virginia, Tennessee, Kentucky, and everywhere else the Separate Baptists would migrate. The Baptists were the early backbone of a much larger contingency of colonists who were now cocked back on their haunches and ready to fight for liberty.

The Revolution

The Baptists were not idle during the Revolution. That the Revolution was used by God to produce a nation that would bless the Jew, spread the Gospel, and publish the Word of God is indisputable; that He used His people, the Baptists, to accomplish these ends is also a glaring fact of history.

Baptist Principles of Liberty and Limited Government Fueled the Revolution

The Baptist involvement with a pre-Revolutionary movement, the Regulators, has already been discussed. The fact that the Baptists were hated by Governor Tryon is clear. The fact that the Battle of Alamance took place near Sandy Creek, a highly concentrated Baptist area in North Carolina, is also true. The hanging of Benjamin Merrill of Jersey Settlement Baptist Church is a well documented point of record. The principles of liberty fought for in North Carolina were proclaimed far and wide by the Baptists.

Historian William Cathcart puts forth an interesting thesis in his great book *Baptist Patriots and the American Revolution*. Cathcart teaches that the non-Baptist colonists actually learned how to resist tyranny and stand for liberty from the often persecuted Baptists. The principles that the whole would embrace and fight for were simply the principles the Baptists for decades had fought for by themselves. Consider the following points as evidence of this idea.

Baptists Demanded Liberty Long Before the Revolution

They were fined, beaten, banished, and disfranchised repeatedly by oppressive colonial governments and yet protested and endured without wavering. Cathcart stated the following:

> In June, 1768, John Waller, Lewis Craig and James Childs, three Baptist ministers were arrested in Spotsylvania County, Virginia, on the charge of "preaching the gospel contrary to law." "May it please your worship," said the prosecuting attorney, "they cannot meet a man on the road without ramming a text of Scripture down his throat." On refusing to pledge themselves to stop preaching in that county for a year and a day, they were forthwith ordered to prison.
>
> (*Baptist Patriots and the American Revolution*, p. 18)

As the colonists witnessed this spirit, it taught them the same. Again Cathcart says,

> "William Webber and Joseph Anthony were imprisoned in Chesterfield County for preaching Jesus. And such poor reverence did they cherish for the unjust laws of Virginia that they actually invited the people to come to the walls of the jail that they might proclaim to them the good news of the kingdom" (Ibid, p. 19).

The Portsmouth Compact and Rhode Island Charter were Baptist documents.
These early laws were covered in this study in a previous chapter. They were produced long before

the Revolution and these documents granted liberty to all. Cathcart stated:

> Before the Revolution Rhode Island was the freest Colony in North America, or in the history of our race. Her Baptist founders had made their settlement a Republic complete in every development of liberty, even while under the nominal rule of a king; they created a government with which there could be no lawful interference by any power in the Old World or the New.

(*Baptist Patriots and the American Revolution*, p. 26)

From the Battle of Alamance to the beating of Obadiah Holmes, and from the pulpit of John Clarke to the prisons in Virginia, the Baptists for over one hundred thirty years were an excellent example of patriotism and liberty for all men. This example spread throughout the colonies and influenced others. We agree with Cathcart when he said, "The Baptists gave the colonists of America an impressive example of disobedience to wicked laws."

The Baptists supported the Continental Congress.
The first Continental Congress assembled on September 5, 1774. The Baptists were among the earliest religions to support it. The New England Baptists of the Warren Association, eight days after

the origination of the Continental Congress, declared it the supreme court of the American colonies and said that they were "…willing to unite with our dear countrymen to pursue every prudent measure for relief" (quote from Isaac Backus). The Philadelphia Baptist Association supported the Continental Congress as well.

The Baptists took their place on the battlefields.
   The Virginian historian Howison stated,

> "No class of the people of America were more devoted advocates of the principles of the Revolution, none were more willing to give their money and goods to their country, none more prompt to march to the field of battle, and none more heroic in actual conflict than the Baptists of Virginia"

(*Baptist Patriots and the American Revolution*, p. 66).

The Battle of King's Mountain
   On October 7, 1780, a mostly Baptist contingent, affectionately remembered as the "Overmountain Men," defeated a British force at King's Mountain. These men came from Virginia, North Carolina, South Carolina, Georgia, and what would later become Tennessee. The latter group, a largely Baptist group of frontiersmen, walked almost nonstop for over eleven days to this battle. The impor-

tance of their victory is recorded by Jeffrey J. Crow in his *Chronicle of North Carolina during the American Revolution*.

> In response to the impudent threat, frontiersmen from Virginia, North Carolina, South Carolina, Georgia, and what later became Tennessee joined forces to attack the British army. Ferguson retreated to King's Mountain and camped atop its steep slopes, some one-and-one-half miles from the North Carolina border. In a brilliant four-pronged attack, the undisciplined and untrained militia captured the mountain while inflicting heavy losses on the enemy. Ferguson was killed. The victory was all the more remarkable because the military force had proceeded without the leadership or guidance of the state or of the Continental Line (p. 43).

Baptist Chaplains

Baptist preachers from numerous locations were zealous in their desire to serve as chaplains. John Gano, Hezekiah Smith, and Charles Thompson to name a few, served faithfully in this capacity. George Washington once stated that "Baptist chaplains were among the most prominent and useful in the army" (Manning and Brown University, p. 136, Boston: 1864). He certainly held at least one chaplain in the highest possible regard—his personal chaplain, John Gano.

The Baptist Baptism of George Washington

It is important for Baptists to be given a record of the following historical fact. The devil has kept it from Baptists for far too long. The fact is this: General George Washington was saved and baptized at the conclusion of the Revolution. His personal chaplain administered the sacred ordinance. In a letter written by General Richard Gano, grandson of Chaplain John Gano, he stated the following:

General Washington on one occasion said to Chaplain Gano:

> "I am convinced that immersion is the baptism taught in the Scriptures, and I demand baptism at your hands."

> (Beller, *America In Crimson Red*, p. 295)

Beller also submitted several sworn affidavits as evidence of this fact. Consider just one:

> Georgetown, KY., Aug. 16th, 1889
> To Whom It May Concern:
>
> I, Margaret Ewing (nee Gano) age 90 years last May, being of sound mind and memory, make this statement; I have often heard my Aunt Margaret Hubbell (nee Gano), the eldest daughter of Rev. John Gano say that her father told her that he baptized General George Washington, at Valley Forge to the

best of my recollection. She, Mrs. Hubbell, also said that General Washington, for prudent reasons, did not desire that his baptism should be made public. Rev. John Gano was a Chaplain in the Revolutionary War, and an intimate personal friend of General Washington.

Margaret Ewing,
Subscribed and sworn to in my presence this 16th day of August 1889.
Stephen G. Long, Notary Public, State of Kentucky

For the full record, see Dr. James Beller's *America in Crimson Red,* pages 294-301. It is great for Baptist Christians to know that the influence of the Baptists on the Revolution reached so far and wide that their spiritual power touched even the heart of General George Washington, the father of our country!

Review Questions

1. The Separate Baptists were being used of God to sew the _____ _____ of a nation.

2. The influence of the Baptists on the _____ is almost wholly unknown.

3. If you take the Separate Baptists out of the picture, _____ would be a different place spiritually.

4. If you would take away the _____ influence on the Revolution, there would probably not be an America today.

5. William Cathcart said, "Baptists have ever been the ardent friends of _____ and _____ liberty.

6. The _____ Act, the _____ Act, and the _____ Act angered the colonists and stirred them to rebellion.

7. Governor _____ _____ quickly became an enemy of Baptists.

8. Tryon's subordinates kept over _____ of the taxes they collected.

9. Those who opposed Gov. Tryon were known as the "_____."

10. After losing the Battle of _____, Capt. Benjamin _____ and five others were hanged in Hillsborough, North Carolina.

Lesson Six

11. Name three churches that Gov. Tryon wreaked havoc on after Alamance.

_____,
_____,
_____.

12. The Baptist Regulators paved the way for the _____ _____.

13. Cathcart taught that the non-Baptists learned how to resist _____ from the Baptists.

14. The Baptists were one of the earliest religious groups to support the Continental _____.

15. The mostly Baptist "Overmountain Men" won a decisive victory over the British at the Battle of _____ _____.

16. George Washington once stated that "_____ chaplains were among the most prominent and useful in the army."

17. General George Washington was saved and _____ at the conclusion of the Revolution.

18. General Washington once said to Chaplain Gano: "I am convinced that _____ is the baptism taught in the Scriptures, and I demand baptism at your hands."

19. The fuller record of Washington's baptism can be found in Beller's book _____ _____ _____ _____.

20. The truth about Washington's baptism has been hidden by the _____ for far too long.

Lesson Seven

The Virginia Baptists, a Rare Breed

…We ought to obey God rather than men.
Acts 5:29b

In lesson five we examined Shubal Stearns, the Sandy Creek Baptist Church, and the great Separate Baptist Revival. We then moved into lesson six where we learned that the Sandy Creek Church and several other churches in North Carolina were reduced in number and strength considerably. Governor Tryon and his cohorts hurt Baptist expansion in North Carolina for around an hundred years.

In lesson seven we will turn our attention to Virginia. It is important to point out that while North Carolina was declining due to the War of Regulation, the light of the Gospel was beginning to break forth with great power in other places. In no place was this more evident than in Virginia. The Baptist revival that started in North Carolina and was centered there for several years would soon be transplanted in Virginia. For many years Virginia would become a place of revival and growth for the Baptists. Morgan Edwards recorded a vision that God gave to Brother Shubal Stearns. This vision is recorded below. It took place during a great storm two years prior to Stearns' death.

> As Stearns was ascending a hill not far from his home, he saw on the horizon "a white heap like snow." As he approached the formation, which appeared to be suspended fifteen or twenty feet above ground, the mass suddenly fell to the ground and broke into three parts. The greatest part moved northward, a second part southward, and the third "less than either but much brighter" remained in the spot where it fell. Stearns watched first the northern part and then the southern as they vanished. Then after he had pondered the meaning of what he had seen, he decided that, "the bright heap is our religious interest; which will divide and spread north and south, but chiefly northward; while a small part remains at Sandy Creek." (Lumpkin, p. 87)

Although we are careful when dealing with "visions," we know that God speaks to men, and we also know that this "vision" came to pass. Virginia would play a significant role in perpetuating both revival and liberty in America.

Because of the Anglican state-church mentality in Virginia, Baptists were looked on as charlatans by many. Lies were concocted and fear ensued among many of the common people. Some had heard that Baptist preachers were magicians with the power to

Lesson Seven

grab people through their preaching and publicly embarrass them. Their unorthodoxy, loudness, unusual gestures, and zeal caused many to reject them off hand.

It seems as though after some time, God began to breathe upon the Virginia Baptists and their work and preaching, as He had done in North Carolina. By the late 1760s sentiments began to change. In fact, as early as 1759 it is recorded by Ryland that one Anglican minister stated, *"Wherever the Baptists appeared the people flocked over to them."*

As true as this is, it is interesting to note that the Anglicans were not happy about this. In fact, as soon as the Baptists began to flourish in Virginia, the state-church brought down an iron fist of oppression.

By the time the smoke cleared in old Virginia, the Baptists had birthed numerous churches, won thousands of converts, secured a Bill of Rights and religious liberty for a nation, and ultimately carried faithfully the revival torch handed them by Brother Shubal Stearns.

These Virginia Baptists were a rare breed for sure. It is the intention of the author, in this lesson, to highlight a few of these Baptist ministers with the purpose of gaining a fuller appreciation for their dedication and our religious liberty.

John Leland

John Leland was born in May of 1754 in Grafton, Massachusetts. Little did his parents know, but this unsuspecting child would grow to be a mighty man of God. He would eventually sit before dignitaries and magistrates and righteously pour forth the words of liberty that would shape a nation. He was Virginia's greatest preacher/statesman. He has been called an "apostle of religious and political liberty" (Dalton).

In 1774 he was converted at the age of twenty. He was baptized by Noah Alden, who was baptized by Shubal Stearns. Soon after, he traveled to Virginia because he felt called of God to preach the Gospel, to battle the state-church, and to establish religious liberty. William Cathcart records his success as a preacher in Virginia. He had "3009 sermons preached, 700 persons baptized, and two large churches formed, one of 300 members, and another of 200." In addition to this, while he was in Virginia, he traveled approximately 75,000 miles in itinerant evangelism.

Although his numerous converts, baptisms, and pastorates are notable, it is his involvement in the battle for religious liberty that is most noteworthy. The battle he helped to win would ensure religious liberty for thousands of others to preach the Gospel. The liberty he won would allow millions to both hear the Gospel and be saved.

Liberty of Conscience

He was a noble defender of every man's conscience, as John Clarke, Roger Williams, and Obadiah Holmes were before him. His sentiments on Christians, submitting their consciences to the state in any way, can be summed up in the following statement:

> If a creed of faith, established by law, was ever so short, and ever so true; if I believed the whole of it with all my heart—should I subscribe to it before a magistrate, in order to get indulgence, preferment, or even protection—I should be guilty of a species of idolatry, by acknowledging a power, that the Head of the Church, Jesus Christ, has never appointed. (Leland)

Leland's definition of liberty of conscience was made plain by the preacher himself. He stated, "I mean the inalienable right that each individual has of worshipping his God according to the dictates of his conscience, without being prohibited, directed, or controlled therein by human law, either in time, place, or manner."

Opposition from State Sponsored Religion and from the World

Not only was Leland imprisoned, but he also faced angry mobs at times. One time, when administering baptism to a new convert, he faced the fury of her unconverted husband. He stated,

> "In the south part of Orange [County] a man took his gun with the profession to kill me. He had given his consent for his wife to be baptized, and the meeting was appointed for that purpose; but when we got to the place, and I had taken her by the hand to lead her into the water, there was an alarm that the man was coming with his gun. While a detachment of the congregation went to meet the man, to pacify him, I thought, 'Now, or never,' and baptized her. No mischief ensued."

These incidents only aided in emboldening him.

Leland and the Bill of Rights

Leland traveled far and wide preaching the Gospel and proclaiming the need for liberty of conscience. David Cummins stated of Leland,

> "He was a neighbor of James Madison and Thomas Jefferson. Being very active in the political arena, he not only expressed Baptist views of liberty of conscience but he rallied the Baptists in support of James Madison as a delegate to the Virginia Constitutional Convention and later in his election to the House of Representatives. Madison had promised the Baptists that if elected, he would introduce a bill of rights early in the first session of Congress."

The Constitution did not guarantee an individual right of liberty of conscience. Therefore, Leland could not endorse it or Madison as a delegate to the Virginia Constitutional Convention without a guarantee of a future Bill of Rights outlining this particular.

James Madison Seeks out Leland's Support

Leland held such sway among the largely Baptist populace of Virginia that Madison became concerned for his political future. He knew he would not be elected unless he could persuade Leland to endorse him. James Madison met with Leland; and after hearing Leland's reasoning for a Bill of Rights, he agreed with Leland. He then promised the Baptist preacher that if he would secure the Baptist vote for his election, one day he would introduce a Bill of Rights on the floor of the U. S. Congress. This promise he kept!

The first amendment is on the books because of the fearless stand of the Virginia Baptists, led by the Baptist preacher John Leland. Joseph Dawson in *Baptists and the American Republic* said, "The first amendment was the fulfillment by Madison of a promise made to the Baptist evangelist John Leland and the Baptists in Virginia."

Leland Goes Home

Having finished the spiritual and political work

God had called him to in Virginia, John Leland traveled home to Cheshire, Massachusetts, in 1792. There he continued to preach and pastor. He also stumped for Thomas Jefferson in his successful bid for the 1801 presidency.

The Big Cheese

Leland believed that America finally had a "people's president." He believed that Thomas Jefferson was for the common citizen. He and his congregation celebrated when Jefferson won, esteeming him as one who was a "friend to liberty," both political and religious.

To show their gratitude and love for Jefferson,

> "One day all of the milk from 900 local, loyal Republican cows was collected and brought into Cheshire, where the population gathered to sing hymns, socialize, and make cheese. The product of this effort was a mammoth cheese wheel four feet, four and one-half inches in diameter, fifteen inches thick, and weighing 1,235 pounds!" (Cummins, *This Day in Baptist History Vol. 1*, p. 66).

Leland, with some help, personally delivered the cheese to Jefferson in Washington, D. C. Jefferson affectionately welcomed the Baptists, accepted the gift, and became another part of history by receiving the original "Big Cheese!"

Lesson Seven

Souls, His Driving Motivation

John Leland labored for 67 years. He considered the "salvation of the soul" his highest priority. Greene records Leland's sentiments as such, "For forty years, next to the salvation of the soul, the rights of conscience have been articles of my highest solicitude."

John Leland's Self Written Epitaph

"Here lies the body of John Leland, who labored 67 years to promote piety and vindicate the civil and religious rights of all men."

Samuel Harriss

As we consider Separate Baptist expansion and success in Virginia, it is impossible to go far before we must stop to consider the "Apostle of Virginia," Samuel Harriss. Colonel Samuel Harriss was born in Hanover County, Virginia, in January of 1724. Early on he showed himself a leader, serving in many capacities including sheriff, justice of the peace, and colonel of the militia.

Salvation

Harriss was visiting some forts, dressed in full military garb, when he decided to stop to hear Joseph and William Murphy preach. As he listened to the "Murphy boys" preach and exhort, he fell under deep conviction. Hiding himself behind a nearby loom in the house did no good. Soon he cast off his sword and other military pieces and prostrated himself over a pew. When he was saved, he arose shouting, "Glory, glory, glory!"

Preaching

Harriss was baptized by Daniel Marshall. He joined Dutton Lane's church and began to labor zealously. Harriss copied Marshall's tones and gestures while preaching. He went everywhere preaching the Gospel. The power of God was all over his ministry. Semple relates that the excellency of his preaching lay chiefly in "addressing the heart" and that "perhaps even Whitefield did not surpass him in this. He was a man of the greatest personal force. He seldom failed to stir an audience, his eyes appearing to pour forth 'streams of celestial lightning' which whithersoever he turned his face, would strike down hundreds at once." People would sometimes fall flat under his preaching. Multitudes met God under his ministry.

Church Planter

> "Harriss had the assistance of several North Carolina itinerants in planting the earliest Separate churches in south central Virginia. The Dan River Church was constituted in 1760 by Daniel Marshall and Philip Mulkey. There were 74 charter members...includ-

Lesson Seven 137

ing Harriss, Dutton Lane, Thomas Hargat, and their wives" (Lumpkin, 90).

Opposition

Harriss was opposed often in his ministry. He saw clubs, sticks, and whips at some of his meetings.

> "Like Daniel Marshall, Harriss possessed a spirit incapable of being discouraged by any difficulty. While preaching in Orange County, Harriss was pulled down, dragged about sometimes by his hair and sometimes by his leg. On another occasion he was knocked down by a rude fellow. He went to preach to the prisoners in the town of Hillsborough, where they locked him up for a considerable time" (Cummins).

His ministry may best be summed up by one who knew him well, James Ireland. He said the following about Samuel Harriss:

> I saw him ordained and a moving time it was. He was considered a great man in the things of time and sense; but he shone more conspicuously in the horizon of the church, during the time of our sweet intercourse together, so that he was like another Paul among the churches. No man like minded with him, who like a blazing comet, would rush through the colony or state displaying the banners of his adorable Master, spreading His light and diffusing His

heat to the consolation of thousands (Little, *Imprisoned Preachers*).

Lewis Craig

Lewis Craig was born in Orange County, Virginia, around 1737. James B. Taylor relates:

> This is a name well known in Virginia. It is interwoven in the history of many of her churches, and will continue to live in the memory of the pious, while time endures. To Lewis Craig and his brother Elijah, may we look as among the principal instruments of introducing the gospel, in the eastern part of our state (*Lives of Virginia Baptist Ministers*, p. 116).

God first worked in his heart as he heard Samuel Harriss preach. After hearing him on several occasions, he was saved. He was baptized at age 27 and began to preach. He traveled extensively and had large crowds often in attendance. He was a tremendous preacher who had hundreds of converts. Spencer had this to say of Craig:

> As an expositor of the Scriptures, [Lewis Craig] was not very skillful, but dealt closely with the heart. He was better acquainted with men than with books. He never dwelt much on doctrine, but mostly on experimental and practical godliness. Though he was not called a great preacher, perhaps there was never found in Kentucky so great a gift of exhortation as

in Lewis Craig. The sound of his voice would make men tremble and rejoice. The first time I heard him preach, I seemed to hear the sound of his voice for many months (*History of the Kentucky Baptists, Vol. 1*, p. 31-32).

A Successful Ministry Shrouded by Persecution
His labors included helping plant the first Baptist church between the Rappahannock and James Rivers. He became pastor of this church and pastored there until 1781. Before long, Lewis Craig would be arrested on more than one occasion. Cathcart tells us that upon one arrest he, John Waller, and James Childs were being transported from the courthouse to the jail. As they went they sang a hymn to the magistrates, "Broad is the Road that Leads to Death." He often preached through the jail bars. His soulwinning zeal greatly offended the sheriff of Spottsylvania. The prosecuting attorney once stated of he and his fellow preachers that, "They cannot meet a man upon the road but they must ram a text of Scripture down his throat."

Around 1770, Patrick Henry rode sixty miles on horseback to secure the release of Lewis, Joseph Craig and Aaron Bledsoe. This he did while pleading in court for liberty. They were released (John Mason Peck).

Other Labors

Semple relates that Tuckahoe, Upper King and Queen, and Upper Essex churches in the Dover Association were planted under his ministry.

Traveling Church

Lewis Craig was a great influence in Virginia; however, he was also burdened with the souls out West. In September of 1781 Lewis Craig led the vast majority of his church to depart Virginia and carry the Gospel to the new country called Kentucky. After saying their sad farewells and loading up the wagons, they departed. Over 600 people made the long, hard journey southwest, through the Cumberland Gap and then swinging back northwest. They landed near Gilbert's Creek in north central Kentucky. They had gone 600 miles in about 4 months. In December of 1781, on the second Sunday, they had their first worship service in the area many of them would call home. Craig established the South Elkhorn Church in 1783 and the South Elkhorn Association. He further birthed the Bracken Baptist Church in Minerva, Kentucky, as well as others.

> He lived to advanced age. His last days were distinguished by increased spirituality of mind. His conversation was mostly on heavenly topics, and it was frequently said that he seemed to enjoy much of heaven in his soul. His trials had been greatly sanc-

tified to his good, and like a little child he yielded quietly to the will of his Father. He died, after a short illness, in the 87th year of his age.

(Taylor, *Lives of Virginia Baptist Ministers*, p. 122)

James Ireland

James Ireland was born in Edinburgh, Scotland, in 1748. He was brought up in a Presbyterian home. He came to America as a young man and was quickly overtaken by sin. He once stated,

> "I could soon join in the wicked amusements of those around me without remorse, and being of an aspiring disposition, it did not suit my taste, to be a common accomplice with them, but an active leader in all their practices of wickedness" (Taylor, p. 159).

When he was saved, he wept for "several hours." He was the first person baptized by Samuel Harriss.

When he began to preach, God's blessing was evident on him. He was instrumental in forming several churches that were in the Ketocton Association.

James Taylor (*Lives of Virginia Baptist Ministers*, p. 170) said,

> "Several hundreds were by him led into the watery

tomb, expressive of their death unto sin. In 1802, he baptized, in one of his churches, ninety-three persons, fifty-two of whom were received in one day."

He was opposed on every hand. While imprisoned for preaching, he was almost killed in a "gun powder" plot. The gun powder tore up some of his cell floor, but he was divinely protected. Attempts to poison and suffocate him also failed. There was an unusual hatred for him and his preaching, and he once stated that "he might speak of a hundred instances of cruelty which were practiced." Through it all, he maintained a good spirit and confidence in God. His custom was to sign his letters from prison with the words, "from my palace in Culpepper."

> "His persecutions permanently injured his health; two accidents completed the work begun by state-church tyranny, and Mr. Ireland entered his rest May 5, 1806" (Cathcart, *Baptist Encyclopedia, Vol. 1*, p. 585).

Other Imprisoned Preachers in Virginia
John Waller

John Waller was once known as "Swearing Jack Waller." He was on the grand jury when Lewis Craig was tried in court. Craig said this to the grand jury:

> "I thank you, gentlemen of the grand jury, for the

honour you have done me. While I was wicked and injurious, you took not notice of me; but since I have altered my course of life, and endeavored to reform my neighbors, you concern yourselves much about me. I forgive my persecuting enemies, and shall take joyfully the spoiling of my goods." When Mr. Waller heard him speak in that manner, and observed the meekness of his spirit, he was convinced that Craig was possessed of something that he had never seen in the man before. He thought within himself, that he should be happy if he could be of the same religion with Mr. Craig. (David Benedict)

The state-church hated Waller because of his vibrant testimony of a changed life and because he had betrayed the state-church officials by leaving their ranks and becoming a Baptist. Benedict records:

A very great revival commenced under Mr. Waller's ministry, in 1787. In this revival he was greatly engaged; and baptized from first to last many hundreds, and his church in a short time increased to about 1500 members. November 8th, 1793, moved his family to Abbeville district, in the State of South Carolina. This removal was said to [come] from a strong desire to live near a beloved daughter, who had married Rev. Abraham Marshall, of Georgia. He remained faithful in the cause, until his death, July 4th, 1802.

John Weatherford

John Weatherford had been imprisoned in the Chesterfield County jail of the colony of Virginia for five months in the year 1773. Like his brethren, Weatherford preached through the grates of the prison. The opponents of Weatherford and his Baptist friends would stand by the window and slash his hands with knives causing the blood to run down the walls of the prison.

After being held in close prison for some time, Weatherford was allowed the privilege of the prison bounds. Sometime later an order for his release was secured. The jailer refused to free Weatherford until the jail fees (room and board) were paid, which amounted to a considerable sum because of the length of his imprisonment. Not long afterward, this fee was paid by someone whose name was concealed, and Weatherford was released. More than twenty years later, Patrick Henry moved to Charlotte County and became a neighbor to John Weatherford, who was pastoring a nearby Baptist church. It was not until this time, in discussing their early experiences in the fight for liberty, that Pastor Weatherford learned for the first time that Patrick Henry had paid his fine and brought about his release. Of course Weatherford never lost his love and admiration for Patrick Henry.

Lesson Seven

During his last illness, he would often try to win the lost from his bedside. Each day towards the end of his life, he requested "Amazing Grace" to be sung. John Weatherford went to his eternal reward on January 23, 1833. He was more than ninety years of age.

(Little, *Imprisoned Preachers and Religious Liberty in Virginia*, p. 358)

In Virginia over forty Baptist preachers were jailed before the Revolutionary War. Their struggles produced a nation where no one would be imprisoned for obeying their conscience. Today, we salute this "Rare Breed."

Review Questions

1. _____ would play a significant role in perpetuating both revival and liberty in America.

2. Because of the Anglican state-church mentality in Virginia, Baptists were looked on as _____ by many.

3. _____ _____ was Virginia's greatest preacher/statesman.

4. John Leland was called an "apostle of _____ and _____ liberty."

5. John Leland was a noble defender of every man's _____.

6. _____ _____ sought out Leland's support.

7. John Leland considered the "_____ of the _____" his highest priority.

8. Samuel Harriss was called the "_____ of _____."

9. As he listened to the "_____ _____" preach and exhort, Harriss fell under deep conviction.

10. Harriss was baptized by _____ _____.

11. Harriss copied Marshall's _____ and _____ while preaching.

12. Lewis Craig first came under conviction listening to _____ _____ preach.

13. It was said of Lewis Craig that the sound of his voice would make men _____ and _____.

14. As Craig, Waller, and Childs were being transported by the magistrates, they _____ a _____.

15. It was said of him and his fellow preachers that "they cannot meet a man upon the road, but they must ram a text of Scripture _____ _____ _____."

16. _____ _____ rode 60 miles on horseback to secure Craig's release.

17. The Traveling Church consisted of _____ people, traveled _____ miles, and completed their trip in about _____ months.

18. James Ireland was born in_____, _____.

19. Ireland was the first person baptized by
_____ _____.

20. He signed his letters from prison with the words, "_____ ___ _____ ___ _____."

21. Name three ways the state-church tried to do away with James Ireland.
_____
_____
_____

22. John Waller was once known as "_____ _____ _____."

23. As John Weatherford preached through the grates of the prison, his opponents would slash his hands with _____.

Lesson Eight

American Baptist Missions/ American Indian Missions

> So they, being sent forth by the Holy Ghost, departed…
>
> **Acts 13:4a**

Independent Baptists in America did a great work in spreading the Gospel in the 20th century. This is especially evident when compared with the work done in previous centuries. Untold numbers of doctrinally sound, Spirit-filled missionaries have been sent to the four corners of the globe in the last one hundred years.

Not only have we (scriptural Baptists) sent God's servants to the fields in unprecedented numbers, but independent Baptists have translated the Word of God into many foreign tongues with the purpose of reaching the whole world with the gospel. Bible-believing Baptists have shipped pallet after pallet and truckload after truckload of Scripture portions, tracts, and whole Bibles at a rate that the world has never before seen.

We have come to a place where we look at our

missions activity as the norm. Many of us have been giving to missions for a long time. Many Baptists, not just Baptist ministers but the faithful church member, have been on one or more mission trips. Baptist youth groups use mission trips as a normal way to let our young people see the lost world out there, in hopes that the eye might affect the heart.

The truth is that the vast majority of independent Baptists wouldn't join a non-mission supporting church. Thank God for that fact. That is the way it ought to be and that is the way it is. The author is glad to be able to report the above. Missions have truly taken off in recent decades. In fact, all of this is so positive, and God has done such a great work in and through independent Baptists in America, that we only find one downside to the whole thing. The one thing that concerns the author is that we have taken it all for granted. Could it be that we are not thankful to God enough for what **He** has done with American foreign missions? If we are not careful, we will lose God's blessings by simply not acknowledging that **He** has done marvelous things in American missions.

To truly appreciate what God has and is doing with American foreign missions, we must look into what great doctrinal and spiritual barriers He overcame to bring America to the place it is today on the forefront of foreign missions.

Lesson Eight

This lesson will discuss the reasons missions floundered in the early years of our country. It will also show how God broke through those barriers. We will focus on key men and ministries that God used to start American missions. These men must be remembered for their sacrifice and submission to God. It was their foundational work that paved the way in making America what it is today: the largest missions sending country in the history of mankind!

Calvinist England

While America was seeing steady Baptist growth in the 18th century, England was not. This is due to one thing and one thing alone. As America was filling up with Separate Baptists who were extremely evangelistic and could in no way be called "hyper-Calvinist," England was being overrun by hyper-Calvinist extremes. The evangelistic Separates flourished in America, and the Particular and General Baptists were quite populous in England. These latter groups, especially the Particular Baptists, were hyper-Calvinistic. Their theology dictated their practice, and England began to wilt.

England had by the year 1800, about 36,000 Particular Baptists represented by 361 churches as documented by the historian Benedict. These churches were represented by nine associations, which were steeped in hyper-Calvinism. Their most outspoken champion in the Calvinist school was a London pastor named John Gill. He was a prolific writer and held great sway with the Particular Baptists of England. Gill taught that it was wrong to publicly invite sinners to Christ.

Light Breaks Forth in England

One man that Gill influenced was John Ryland. Ryland had pastored first in Northampton in 1781, and then the famous Broadmead Baptist Church in 1791. He was a leader in the Northamptonshire Baptist Association.

> It was at the Northamptonshire Association meetings that William Carey and Andrew Fuller spoke out on the need to take the Gospel to the people of eastern Asia. At one juncture Mr. Ryland, marked with hypercalvinism, told Carey, "Sit down young man, when the Lord gets ready to convert the heathen, he will do it without your help or mine!" Thankfully, Ryland later had a change of heart.
>
> (Beller, *Collegiate Baptist History Workbook*, p. 230)

American Baptist Missions — The Stage is Set
William Carey and Andrew Fuller

We introduce William Carey and Andrew Fuller here, not because they were great American missionaries, but rather because the fire they lit, by opposing hyper-Calvinist extremes in England, would spread to America. Baptists in America owe much to these men.

William Carey was born in Purey, Northampton, England, in 1761. He was born an Episcopalian, but was saved and later baptized in 1783 after becoming a Baptist through reading his Bible. Carey had an amazing mind; and according to William Cathcart, he learned Latin, Greek, Hebrew, French, and Dutch in only seven years. "In reading the voyages of the celebrated Captain Cook, he first had his attention directed to the heathen world, and especially to its doomed condition" (Cathcart). He began to write, pastor, and win souls. His famous pamphlet was entitled, "An Inquiry into the Obligation of Christians to Use Means for the Conversion of the Heathen."

His most famous and effective sermon may have been the one he preached at an associational meeting at Nottingham in May of 1792. The message was entitled, "Expect Great Things from God, Attempt Great Things for God."

Andrew Fuller, a pastor at Kettering, was affected by Carey's preaching. At Fuller's church in October of 1792, the first Baptist missionary society in modern times was founded. Its sole purpose was to get the gospel to the heathen.

Carey's field would be India. His accomplishments are best summed up below by Cathcart:

> Carey was the author of a Mahratta grammar, and of a Sanscrit grammar, extending over more than a thousand quarto pages, a Punjabi grammar, a Telinga grammar, and of a Mahratta dictionary, a Bangali dictionary, a Bhotanta dictionary, and a Sanscrit dictionary, the manuscript of which was burned before it was printed. He was also the author of several other secular works. The versions of the Sacred Scriptures appeared in six of these tongues. The New Testament appeared in 23 languages. Carey and his brethren rendered the Word of God accessible to one-third of the world. And even this is not all: before Carey's death 212,000 copies of the Scriptures were issued from Serampore in 40 different languages, the tongue of 330,000,000 of the human family. Dr. Carey was the greatest toolmaker for missionaries that ever labored for God. His versions are used today by all denominations of Christians throughout India.
>
> The first Hindoo convert baptized by Dr. Carey in India was the celebrated Krishna Pal. Dr. Carey founded churches and mission stations in many parts of India, and planted seed from which he gathered precious harvests, and from which his successors have reaped abundantly.
>
> He died June 9, 1834, in his seventy-third year—**the father of modern missions.**
>
> (*Baptist Encyclopedia*, Vol. 1, p. 182-184)

Andrew Fuller was the first secretary of the above mentioned missionary society. Again Cathcart summarizes Fuller's role in missions:

> He traveled all over England very many times, pleading for foreign missions; five times he journeyed through Scotland on the same errand of love; and he visited Ireland once to advocate the cause of the perishing. The noblest cause that stirred up Christian hearts, the cause that brought the Saviour himself from the heavens, found in Andrew Fuller its grandest champion, and to him more than to any other human being was the first foreign missionary society of modern times indebted for its protection in infancy, and the nurturing influences that gave it the strength of a vigorous organization.

(*Baptist Encyclopedia, Vol. 1*, p. 420-422)

Missions Catch on in America
Adoniram Judson

As William Carey is remembered affectionately as the "father of modern foreign missions," Judson should be remembered as the "father of American foreign missions." That the American missionary Adoniram Judson was stirred by the revival of missions in England, led by Carey and Fuller, is indisputable. Baptist historian James Beller stated simply, "Carey's work influenced the American Adoniram Judson" (*America in Crimson Red*, p. 359). Judson, on his way to Carey's field of Burma, as a Congregational minister, was convicted his baptism was illegitimate. He was studying the Scriptures so as to defeat Carey and other Baptists in debates over the subject. His study backfired, and he became a Baptist by conviction. Upon arriving in Burma, he and his wife Ann were scripturally immersed by Carey (according to Cathcart). He then wrote a letter to the Third Congregational Church in Plymouth, explaining his doctrinal change:

> I knew that I had been sprinkled in infancy, and that this had been deemed baptism. But throughout the whole New Testament I could find nothing that looked like sprinkling, in connection with the ordinance of Baptism. It appeared to me, that if a plain person should, without any previous information on the subject, read through the New Testament, he would never get the idea, that baptism consisted in sprinkling. He would find that baptism, in all the cases particularly described, was administered in rivers, and the parties are represented as going down into the water, and coming up out of the water, which they would not have been so foolish as to do for the purpose of sprinkling.
>
> In regard to the word itself which is translated baptism, a very little search convinced me that its plain, appropriate meaning was immersion or dipping; and though I read extensively on the subject, I could not find that any learned Pedobaptist had ever been able

to produce an instance, from any Greek writer, in which it meant sprinkling, or any thing but immersion, except in some figurative applications, which could not be fairly brought into the question.

(Wayland, *A History of the Life and Labors of the Rev. Adoniram Judson,* p. 102-103)

Judson's labors were great. After Judson was dropped by the Congregationalists, Luther Rice led a group of Baptists in sending out missionaries. The Baptist Triennial Convention was formed and supported Judson. Judson's ministry was prosperous and yet was embroiled in sorrow and opposition. Two of his wives died as a result of the severe nature of the mission field. Only his third wife outlived him. Although imprisoned, stricken with sickness, subjected to harsh travel arrangements, ridiculed by enemies, and discouraged by the tragic death of his 2-year old daughter, Judson still did a monumental work in Burma.

He started works in several locations. In addition to this, he labored hard and completed the translation of the Burmese Bible in 1834. On a return trip to America, he took his journey to glory. He died aboard ship on April 12, 1850. James Didier, in his introduction to the book *The Three Mrs. Judsons* relates the following:

Except for the adulation shown for "Old Hickory," Andrew Jackson, Adoniram Judson was, by mid-nineteenth century accounts, the best known and most highly respected national hero of that time. Based upon Judson's letters to his supporters, his tortuous Burmese odyssey had been serialized in newspapers from coast to coast. Though not a Jacksonian frontiersman, Judson created his own frontier. While a firm advocate for the "faith once delivered to the saints," he expanded evangelistic traditions and pushed hard against certain ecclesiastical restraints of his time. He established a clear path for hundreds—even thousands—to travel in his pioneering steps. More than any other figure, he set in motion and energized the missionary movement that captured the imagination of the next several generations and that brought the gospel of Christ to the intersections of what was then referred to as the provinces of the heathen. (Didier, p. xi)

Luther Rice

Luther Rice is one of the most unsung Baptist heroes of all time. His work and accomplishments, if fully examined, would impress the mind of any honest observer. Rice was born in Northborough, Massachusetts, in 1783. He was reared in a Congregational church; but like Judson, he too would become a Baptist by conviction of the Scriptures. While attending Williams College in Massachusetts, he wrote a letter on March 18, 1811, and stated his

Lesson Eight

life's goal: "I have deliberately made up my mind to preach the gospel to the heathen." It seems that God saw his heart and gave him his desires. Like Judson, after Rice came to Baptist convictions, he found himself out in the cold. In September of 1813 the Congregationalists were not pleased with his newfound convictions and severed ties with him.

Rice then invested his efforts with the General Convention of the Baptist Denomination in the United States for Foreign Missions. According to Cathcart, Rice traveled 7,800 miles, collected nearly $3,700, and aroused a warm interest in missions everywhere. These journeys were "through the wilderness and over rivers, across mountains and valleys, in heat and cold, by day and by night, in weariness and painfulness, and fastings and loneliness." This testimonial he reported at the Triennial Convention in Philadelphia in 1817.

He spent his life supporting missionaries, stirring up others to do the same, and preaching the glorious gospel. The eloquent words inscribed on his tomb and other monuments are recorded below as a summary, celebration, and reminder of the useful life of the Baptist minister Luther Rice:

BENEATH THIS MARBLE
Are deposited the Remains of
Elder Luther Rice:

(BORN 25th March A. D. 1783;
DIED 25th September A. D. 1836)
A Minister of Christ, of the Baptist Denomination.
He was a native of Northboro, Massachusetts,
And departed this life, in Edgefield Dist. S. C.
In the death of this distinguished Servant of the Lord
"Is a great Man fallen—in Israel."

Perhaps no American has done more for the great Missionary Enterprise than he. It is thought the first American Foreign Mission, on which he went to India, associated with JUDSON and others, originated with him. And if the BURMANS have cause of gratitude toward JUDSON for a faithful version of GOD'S WORD; so they will, thro generations to come "arise up, and call RICE blessed;" For, it was his eloquent appeals for the HEATHEN, on his return to AMERICA, which roused our Baptist churches to adopt the Burman mission, and sustain JUDSON in his arduous toils. No Baptist has done more for the Cause of Education. He founded "The Columbian College in the District of Columbia," which he benevolently intended, by its Central position, to diffuse knowledge, both literary and religious thro these United States. And if, for want of deserved patronage, that unfortunate institution, which was the special subject of his prayers and toils, for the last Fifteen Years of his life fail to fulfill the high purpose of its founder; Yet, the Spirit of

Lesson Eight

Education awakened by his labors shall accomplish his noble aim.

LUTHER RICE,
With a portly person and commanding presence,
Combined a strong and brilliant intellect.
As a Theologian, he was Orthodox;
A Scholar, his Education was Liberal.
He was an eloquent and powerful Preacher,
A self denying and indefatigable Philanthropist.
His frailties with his dust are entombed
And, upon the WALLS OF ZION, his virtues engraven.
*By order of the BAPTIST Convention,
For the State of S. C.
This MONUMENT is erected*

About a mile from where Rice is buried a historical marker is posted bearing the following inscription:

LUTHER RICE
(1783-1836)
In Pine Pleasant Cemetery, west of
Here, is the grave of Luther Rice,
Prominent Baptist clergyman and
orator who organized American
Baptists on a national scale for

the support of foreign missions and education. He traveled into all parts of the nation in his work, and his personal influence helped shape Baptist history.

American Indian Missions
Isaac McCoy, Getting it Right

Whenever the author does a basic Baptist heritage conference in a local church, it isn't long until the subject of non-Baptist preachers comes up. The sad truth is that many times Baptists recognize the non-Baptists of the past and ignore the Baptists. This has repeatedly been the case. Maybe nowhere has it been as blatant as it has concerning David Brainerd and Isaac McCoy. For many years we have been bombarded with information on Brainerd. In Bible college, in church, and under the preaching of evangelists, we were taught that David Brainerd, the Congregationalist, was the greatest Indian missionary that ever walked on American soil. However, after a thorough, eye-opening study, the author has come to the conclusion that this is one of the biggest misrepresentations that has ever been put forth.

Let the reader understand, the author is not on a crusade to downplay all non-Baptists of the past. Nor does he deny their contributions. However, when one lays the life of Isaac McCoy next to that of David Brainerd, it becomes very evident that it is not even a fair comparison. With all due respect to the memory of Brainerd, his relatively short ministry, with few lasting scriptural accomplishments and only a handful of converts, pales when laid next to the accomplishments of the greatest Indian missionary to ever walk on American soil: one-Isaac McCoy.

The Life of Isaac McCoy

Isaac McCoy was born in Fayette County, Pennsylvania, near Union Town. He was born on June 13, 1784, of Scotch-Irish ancestry. His parents, William and Elizabeth, were Baptists. Isaac had two brothers and two sisters. His father moved the family to Kentucky in the spring of 1789.

Character Instilled

Isaac had a godly mother, who helped to shape his character. He recalled one memory of his mother as such: she "remonstrated against vice and the follies of youth, especially enjoining upon us the duty of prayer…" (Isaac McCoy's family record-1808).

His character was evidenced in various situations as a youth. Once when chopping wood with his brother John, they became careless. The result was two less fingers on Isaac's left hand. Years later he wrote, "Three weeks completely healed this wound but left me ever after to lament my childish folly." It would appear to be normal for Isaac not to blame his brother for the accident. McCoy detested sin, even before he was converted. It has been recorded that at the sound of a violin he would run the other direction for fear of falling into sin.

Salvation

In the year 1800, a great revival swept across Kentucky. McCoy was saved in the midst of this great move of God. He was baptized on March 6, 1801, by Joshua Morris and became a member of the Plum Creek Church. McCoy was married on October 6, 1803, to Christiana Polke.

Labor as a Pastor

The McCoys moved to Indiana in 1804, finally settling in Vincennes, Indiana, in 1809. Early on, McCoy helped form missionary societies in the Maria Creek Church. In January of 1810 he became pastor of the Maria Creek Baptist Church. In addition to preaching, McCoy wrote pamphlets and songs of the faith. The War of 1812 ensued, and the faith of Maria Creek Church was tried. It was said of McCoy that he: "Trusting in God and armed with his Bible and musket, traveled from fort to fort, preaching to the people" (Keith, *History of Maria Creek Church*).

Lesson Eight 165

Both the war and their rugged upbringing in Kentucky prepared the McCoys for their life's work, Indian missions. As McCoy traveled and saw the Indians dying without Christ, he was burdened by God to preach to them.

Indian Missions

The following points are the summary assessments of the life and ministry of McCoy by two Baptist historians.

> From Kentucky across the Ohio, Isaac McCoy was the greatest missionary in the history of America. For 30 years (1816-1846), Baptist missionary Isaac McCoy preached the Gospel to the Indians of the Ohio, Mississippi, and Missouri valleys. He birthed churches among the natives in Kentucky, Indiana, Ohio, Illinois, Michigan, Missouri, Kansas, Nebraska, and Oklahoma.
>
> Sensing evil men within the government were attempting to commit genocide against the people he loved, McCoy lobbied and succeeded in creating reservations for the Indian tribes of the Great Plains.
>
> McCoy was a tireless worker who was used of God to see a large number of Indian chiefs and tribal members brought to a saving knowledge of Christ (Beller).

Isaac McCoy founded two mission stations, one of which was the Carey Mission Station established in 1822 near Niles, Michigan. Concerning his labor at this station, Cathcart wrote the following:

> Mr. McCoy and his wife entered upon this missionary work with all the zeal and strength of faith that characterized the life and labors of Mr. and Mrs. Judson. And their faith did not fail. Deprivations, sicknesses, and sorrows such as but few mortals know were not strangers to them. Mr. McCoy rode hundreds of miles through the wilderness and swam the swollen streams lying on the wet ground at night for the sake of carrying forward his missions.

McCoy's own words on his ministry were thus:

> "With my wife and seven small children, I went into the wilderness, to seek an opportunity of preaching Christ to the Indians, without a promise of patronage from anyone, looking to Heaven for help, and trusting that God would dispose the hearts of some, we knew not who, to give my family bread, while I should give myself wholly to the service of the heathen."

(Taken from *History of Baptist Indian Missions*—1840)

We leave the student with the following words which are etched on the memorial monument placed in Fort Wayne, Indiana, in memory of Isaac McCoy:

Lesson Eight

Isaac McCoy arrived in Fort Wayne on May 15, 1820, and founded its first church and school. He lived among and ministered to various Indian tribes. The McCoys fed, clothed, taught, and lodged the Indians. From Fort Wayne, McCoy journeyed into Michigan where he founded the Carey and Thomas mission stations. The Indian Territory was his idea and he is credited with its formation. He made thirteen trips to Washington to persuade the House and Senate to adopt the plan of colonization. His unselfish devotion and untiring efforts on their behalf saved the Indians from certain extinction. He was known and respected by chiefs and presidents alike. Isaac McCoy died June 21, 1846. His last words were, "Tell the brethren to never let the Indian mission decline." He is buried in Western Cemetery—Louisville, Kentucky.

Review Questions

1. We have come to a place where we look at our _____ activity as the norm.

2. Many of us have been giving to missions for a _____ _____.

3. We are not thankful to God enough for what He has done with American _____ _____.

4. Foreign missions _____ in the early years of our country.

5. While America was seeing steady Baptist growth in the 18th century, _____ was not.

6. While America was filling up with Separate Baptists, England was being overrun by _____ - _____ extremes.

7. Their most outspoken champion in the Calvinist school was a London pastor named _____ _____.

8. Mr. Ryland told Carey, "Sit down young man, when the Lord gets ready to _____ the _____, He will do it without your help or mine!"

9. William Carey and Andrew Fuller lit a fire, by opposing hyper-Calvinist _____ in England.

10. This fire would spread to _____.

Lesson Eight

11. Carey preached a famous sermon entitled, "Expect Great Things from God, _____ Great Things for God."

12. Carey is known as the "Father of _____ _____."

13. Andrew Fuller traveled all over England very many times, _____ for _____ _____.

14. Fuller journeyed through Scotland _____ times.

15. Judson should be remembered as the "father of _____ _____ missions."

16. Judson labored hard and completed the translation of the _____ Bible in 1834.

17. Judson established a clear path for hundreds—even thousands—to travel in his _____ _____.

18. Luther Rice is one of the most _____ Baptist heroes of all time.

19. Rice's personal influence helped shape

_____ _____.

20. If you compare McCoy with _____ _____, there is no comparison.

21. In the year 1800, a great revival swept across _____.

22. McCoy was saved in the midst of this _____ _____ of God.

23. Isaac McCoy preached the Gospel to the Indians of the Ohio, _____, and _____ valleys.

24. McCoy birthed churches among natives in _____, _____, _____, _____, _____, _____, _____, _____, _____.

25. McCoy's efforts saved the Indians from certain _____.

Lesson Nine

The Great Revival of 1800/Baptist Expansion

> And the word of the Lord was published throughout all the region.
> **Acts 13:49**

Up to this point in our study of Baptist history in America, we have only alluded to the subject matter of our present lesson. We stated that Isaac McCoy, while in Kentucky, was saved during the revival of 1800. Although we have not said much about the revival of 1800 to this point, the one statement we have made is representative of two truths that will be discussed at this time.

First, we said that Isaac McCoy was saved during the revival of 1800. This fact is merely representative of the multitudes that were converted and joined the ranks of the Baptists during this spectacular move of God. We know that McCoy became a greatly used servant of God, laboring in God's vineyard to reap the souls of Indians. There were many others saved during this revival that would become useful ministers of God. In addition, there were multitudes saved and added to the Baptist churches, who found the will of God outside of the ministerial ranks, and yet were faithful and well pleasing to the Lord.

The second truth we will examine, which was also foreshadowed in our statement concerning McCoy, is the location of the revival. We stated that McCoy was born again in Kentucky. Kentucky was the focal point of this move of God. The revival began in Kentucky, and no state was affected as greatly as Kentucky.

John Henderson Spencer in *A History of Kentucky Baptists, Vol. 1* introduced the great revival in the following manner (let the reader note the statements concerning its effects on Kentucky):

> The revival of 1800 was one of the most wonderful events of modern times. It appeared more like the sudden conversion of a nation than the regeneration and reformation of individuals. If a traveler had passed through the whole breadth of the settled portions of North America, in 1799, he would have heard the songs of the drunkard, the loud swearing and obscenity of crowds around taverns, and the bold, blasphemous vaunting of infidels, in every village and hamlet. If he had returned in 1801, he would have heard, instead, the proclamation of the gospel to awed multitudes, earnest prayers in the groves and forests, and songs of praise to God, along all the public thoroughfares. While this wonderful religious awakening spread with great rapidity over the entire country, from the Atlantic coast to the

extreme frontier settlements in the Great West, in no other locality was it so deep and powerful as in Kentucky, where the people had been most profane in their every day conversation, and blatant in the coarsest type of infidelity. "Where sin abounded, grace did much more abound." (Spencer, chapter 27)

Spiritual Decline in America

That there was a revival of 1800 at all, presupposes that there was a spiritual deadness among believers. This was the case everywhere before God breathed on America again. The Separate Baptist Revival which began in 1755 in North Carolina had long since slowed to a moderate pace. We already stated that the Sandy Creek revival moved into Virginia, and now even old Virginia was not seeing Baptist growth as it had in the previous decades. Virginia, decimated by a war, was simply holding its own in the late 1700s.

Examples of the Decline

John Taylor, who was a fiery evangelist and church planter, stated:

> I never had been so thoroughly cowed down by discouragement through the course of my ministry as now; though it had been in action for 25 years, and really thought I had better been dead than alive,

for I felt as if Satan had gotten the mastery where I lived; So that I could say from my soul, "Woe is me that I sojourn in Meseck, that I dwell in the tents of Keder!"

(Taylor, *The History of Ten Baptist Churches*, p. 135)

Although it is true that Lewis Craig was still laboring in Kentucky, as well as the famed William Hickman, there was not a flood tide of souls being saved before this revival began. It has been said of Hickman that he "baptized more people than any other minister in Kentucky." He and Lewis Craig together labored neck and neck in a race to birth churches; and yet, the overall state of the churches was one of lethargy.

John Taylor, who twenty years earlier was in the midst of the first Kentucky revival, said of his former church, Clear Creek: "The church had not had a single baptism for seven years."

If this is indicative of the spiritual temperature in Kentucky at the time, they were in desperate need of a breath from God.

The 1800 Revival Begins

The revival of 1800 is also known by some historians as the Second Great Awakening. The revival began in the western part of Kentucky, swept into Tennessee mightily, and blew eastward all the way to the coast.

Some historians state plainly, "The revival began among the Presbyterians" (Spencer). It has also been stated that, "Methodists claim some credit for the start of the great revival in the West" (Beller). The truth is that this type of revival could have only been started by the Holy Ghost of God. While we do not deny that the Presbyterians and Methodists experienced God's reviving and convicting presence in their congregations, we do deny that any group can claim responsibility for such a spiritual awakening. The Lord sent fire from heaven, and this fire fell on the whole of America.

Strange Fire

Before we look at the revival fire that fell on the Baptists in the 1800 Revival, it is important to differentiate between revival fire and strange fire. In some non-Baptist congregations, there was sometimes an inability to differentiate between Holy Spirit control of the believer and emotional extremes. Quite frankly, some of what went on in the Methodist and Presbyterian congregations was excessive at least, and many times it was simply "chaos and confusion."

Their meetings were often accompanied by frenzied screaming, personal singing, running, falling down, sobbing, and shouting. Many times it went on for hours and sometimes all night. There was "the falling exercise…jerks, rolling, running, dancing and barking exercises, and finally…visions and dreams" (Spencer).

By contrast, the Baptists were zealous and yet orderly; often loud, and yet rarely did utter chaos ensue, and yet be labeled "as from the Lord." In the following quote we find that the Baptists would not be swept away doctrinally or emotionally by the chaos and ecumenicalism of the Methodists and Presbyterians.

> The greatest excitement prevailed, at what they called the sacramental meetings. Here the Presbyterians and Methodists "communed together" while the restricted communion principle held by the Baptists would not have permitted engaging in these meetings, had they been otherwise disposed to do so. Their principles and polity have usually disposed the Baptists to avoid union meetings, and, during this revival, as at other times, they held their own meetings, and labored in their own quiet, unpretending way (Spencer).

In spite of some of the previously mentioned extremes, the revival catapulted the Presbyterian and Methodist ranks greatly. The statistics of non-Baptist growth during this timeframe is hard to ascertain precisely and is not our purpose here. Let it suffice to say that in at least one instance approximately 3,000 were saved at one camp meeting, and dozens of converts in a single meeting was common.

The Baptists Visited by God

One of the first recorded moves of God among the Baptists seems to have occurred under the preaching of John Taylor, the evangelist. Taylor, speaking of this meeting at Benjamin Craig's meeting house, said,

> Many of the people tarried all night…one object with them was to converse with me; I never heard the question (What shall we do to be saved?) more prevalent. I felt unworthy to be in the company. About sunrise, I took my leave of this blessed company, I had one secret reason, which was to get by myself and mourn over my own barren soul (Taylor).

Disorderly Excesses Were Rare

The Baptist meetings were more scriptural in practice than that of the pedo-Baptists. Spencer reported, "Among the Baptists in Northern Kentucky, where they were by far the most numerous, the revival began, and continued to its close, in a decorous, orderly manner. In the upper Green River country and East Tennessee, where the Separate Baptists were most numerous, there was more excitement, and some *falling* and *jerking*. In Middle Tennessee (then called West Tennessee), "the strange exercises" did not prevail among the Baptists (Spencer).

Baptists Fanned the Flames

The Baptists of Kentucky labored to promote the revival. S. H. Ford said,

> They preached as they always did, except with more earnestness and prayer; and not a landmark was removed or destroyed in their theology, or church polity, or usages. Among those unostentatious workers who claim no honor, and felt no ruinous inflation, were Baptists, who did more under God, in awakening and guiding the out-gush of religious sentiment that swept over Kentucky and the west than all the New Lights put together.
>
> (*Christian Repository*, December 1856, p. 339)

A lesson such as the one you are reading does not provide ample space to relate the full extent of the "Second Great Awakening." Here we provide just a few more instances that became the norm during this outpouring of the Spirit.

> Monthly, people were buried with Christ in baptism, groups of rejoicing converts of every class. 367 were reported baptized into the church at Bryant's. At Great Crossings, the work was more exten-

sive. The earnest and eloquent Redding preached day and night, and from house to house. Crowds thronged the meeting-house. From the Eagle Hills to Cane Runs, age and infancy, black and white, were aroused, were alarmed, were asking, "What shall we do to be saved?" God's presence and power was among them; like the lightning, like the thunder, it shook, it prostrated, it killed to make alive again; and the beautiful waters of the Elkhorn were parted by the burial in baptism of hundreds who now tread the shores of immortality (Beller).

Baptist Growth in Kentucky

Baptist growth in Kentucky was overwhelming, and when one examines the numbers, it becomes easy to see that this truly was a heaven sent revival. In 1800 the Wilderness Church at Clear Creek baptized 326 people within a single year. Remember, this was the church that Taylor said hadn't had a convert in seven years. In the same year, the Bryant's Church added 367 members. In just the spring and summer of 1801 alone, the South Elkhorn Church, at the time pastored by John Shackleford, baptized 309 people into the membership. The South Elkhorn Church was started by the famed Lewis Craig; but, prior to the revival, had entered a state of slumber. Only six people were baptized in the six years previous to the revival. In 1800 McConnell's Run Church added 156 members to its membership. The

Marble Creek Church added 133 in that same year. God also breathed on the Shawnee Run Church and 300 were added to the rolls during the revival.

In addition to this, the several Baptist associations in Kentucky kept copious records, and the numbers added to the churches, when looked at through the perspective of their associational attachments, is very revealing. The following is a summary of the Baptist associations in Kentucky and the growth they experienced during the revival: In 1800 the Elkhorn Association had 1,663 members, and in 1802 their numbers swelled to 5,310. The Bracken Baptist Association went from 539 to 753 within the same timeframe. Green River Association grew from 400 to 800 in two years, and Tate's Creek tripled in number from 600 to 1,802. The South Kentucky Association grew from 1,000 to 2,383; and the Salem Association more than quadrupled. In 1800 the Salem Association had 564 members in its association, and by 1802 it had 2,521. Therefore, in two years Baptists represented by these associations grew from 4,766 to 13,569.

This revival not only gave growth in the previously discussed years, but it seemed to start the snowball rolling. As you look at the following numbers, you can see not just continued growth but faster growth in the following years. In 1784, there were 309 Baptists in Kentucky. In 1792, there were 3,095 on Baptist membership rolls. In 1802, the number grew to 13,569; and by 1812, there were 22,694 members. In all of this growth, God changed the spiritual landscape of Kentucky drastically.

(Above facts compiled from *American in Crimson Red* and Spencer's *History of Kentucky Baptists*)

Kentucky was not the only state affected. Tennessee, Georgia, North and South Carolina, and Virginia saw God do a magnificent work around the turn of the century. Knoxville, Tennessee, was so flooded by Baptists that it became known as "Baptist Town."

In truth, the revival fires began just prior to 1800 spread from county to county, and state to state, until the whole country felt the heat to some degree. Those revival fires did not die down completely until around 1815!

Learning From History – Important Lessons
Revival Praying - As we read about these amazing events that took place during the "Second Great Awakening," it should drive every believer to his knees. The rapid growth of the Baptists in the early 1800s was incredible; and yet when we look at our declining numbers today in America, it can quickly become discouraging. Our dwindling ranks should

not cause us to lose hope; rather, when we see the condition of the Baptists today, it should cause tears of repentance to flow. Our constant heart's cry should be, "Oh God, breathe on us, like in days of old!"

Faithfulness - The second lesson we can glean from this mighty move of God is one of faithfulness. Many of the Baptist ministers that saw God move mightily in their day, during this revival, labored through a period of drought just before the rain of Heaven fell. Had these men given up their posts, they may not have been able to live through this earth-shaking work of God. We are in a drought right now! As the author travels America, he sees a land that is ripe for revival. In the years from 1995 to 2010, the churches have generally become smaller. At the same time, the cults appear to be flourishing. What can we do? We can all be faithful. We can be faithful in Christian living, faithful in proclaiming the cross, and faithful in praying for revival.

Church Planting – A simply profound concept occurred to the author while writing this manuscript. The thought is this: "God cannot bless a church that does not exist!" As simple as this may seem, it is absolutely imperative that we ponder this thought. Consider what America would be like if there were no scriptural Baptist churches in Kentucky for the Lord to revive and expand. Then go back a little further and consider what America would be like if all the Baptist churches planted during the Separate Baptist Revival had not been planted. History has proven that the Methodist and Presbyterian assemblies have been predominantly useless in helping America come to Christ. What if they were the only ones in Kentucky when revival came in 1800? It is, once again, plain to see the extremely important role Baptist church planting has played in America. Baptist church planters—Stearns, Lane, Harriss, Marshall, Mulke, and Vardeman—are the true heroes in American history. Will we take up the torch, or will we let the fire go out in the U.S.A.?

Review Questions

1. Spencer said, "The revival of _____ was one of the most wonderful events of modern times."

2. That there was a revival of 1800 at all, presupposes that there was a spiritual _____ among believers.

3. John Taylor said, "The church had not had a single baptism for _____ years."

4. The revival of 1800 is also known by some historians as the Second _____ _____.

5. This type of revival could have only been started by the _____ _____ of _____.

6. The Lord sent fire from heaven, and this fire fell on the whole of _____.

7. In some non-Baptist congregations, there was an inability to differentiate between Holy Spirit control and _____ _____.

8. The greatest excitement prevailed, at what they called the sacramental meetings. Here the _____ and _____ "communed together."

9. The revival catapulted the Presbyterian and _____ ranks greatly.

10. One of the first recorded moves of God among the Baptists seems to have occurred under the preaching of John _____.

Lesson Nine

11. The Baptist meetings were more _____ in practice than that of the pedo-Baptists.

12. The Baptists of Kentucky labored to _____ the revival.

13. When one examines the numbers, it becomes easy to see that this truly was a _____ _____ revival.

14. In 1800 the Wilderness Church at Clear Creek baptized _____ people within a single year.

15. In the same year, the Bryant's Church added _____ members.

16. In 1800 the Elkhorn Association had 1,663 members, and in 1802 their numbers swelled to _____.

17. Green River Association grew from _____ to 800 in two years.

18. Tate's Creek tripled in number from 600 to _____.

19. In 1800 the Salem Association had 564 members in its association, and by _____ it had 2,521.

20. In two years Baptists represented by these associations grew from 4,766 to _____.

21. God changed the _____ _____ of Kentucky drastically.

22. Tennessee, _____, North and South Carolina, and _____ saw God do a magnificent work around the turn of the century.

23. Those revival fires did not die down completely until around_____!

24. As we read about these amazing events that took place during the "Second Great Awakening," it should drive every believer to their _____.

25. "God cannot bless a church that does not _____!"

Lesson Ten

Baptist Profiles – Important Pastors, Evangelists, Hymn Writers

---

For your obedience is come abroad unto all *men*…
Romans 16:19a

The author of this study has had the awesome privilege of visiting many Baptist sights over the past several years. Many of these sights are directly connected to the history recorded in the chapters of this book. Many things have been gleaned from these trips over the years. Tears have been shed, prayers have been prayed, and friends have been made, all on visits to America's Baptist history sights. Sometimes, however, the greatest lessons learned on Baptist history trips are the ones you don't expect. On one particular trip, after perusing through old churches and strolling up and down the paths of old cemeteries, a truth entered the ears of the author that will not soon be forgotten. The statement was this: "Just remember, of all the gravestones we viewed of famous men, these were just a sampling of the untold thousands of Baptists who were faithful to God."

The previous information was given to introduce the present subject matter. This lesson will deal with profiles of Baptists that need to at least be mentioned. There are some whose contributions to Baptist history left such profound effects on America that their story simply must be told, even if it is related in an ever so brief biography.

Let the reader keep in mind, however, that even as this chapter attempts to give honorable mention to some more heroes of the Baptist faith, we will still be simply scratching the surface of the multitudes of faithful Baptists that helped shape America; yet no one really knows their names or stories. It would be easy to write volumes on the subject of godly "second men" that have never been recognized. Thousands of preachers' wives could be brought to light if the records were available and the effort was made to write such a history. It is impossible to teach all of America's Baptist history in this study. So, we attempt here to do our best in bringing to light just a few more of the many, many faithful!

Pastors/Evangelists
1. William Hickman
One of the most famous of the pioneer Baptist ministers in Kentucky was born in King and Queen Co., VA, February 4, 1747. He was by early training an Episcopalian and entertained great contempt for the Baptists. During a sermon by the renowned John Waller, in 1770, he was deeply impressed. Af-

ter struggling with his sins and his prejudices about three years, he obtained peace in Christ and was baptized. At this time he lived in Cumberland County. There being few preachers in that region, he, with others, established prayer meetings... In 1784 he removed to Fayette Co., KY, where he preached with great zeal and activity in the surrounding settlements. In 1788 he changed his residence to what is now Franklin County. Here, in the same year, he formed the Forks of Elkhorn Church and was chosen the pastor. From this place he made preaching tours among the settlers, often attended by a guard of soldiers to protect him from the Indians. The new churches he formed were watched over and nurtured until they grew strong and the savages were driven from the country. He was greatly blessed in his ministry. A contemporary supposes that in his day he "baptized more people than any other minister in Kentucky." He probably formed more churches than even the famous Lewis Craig. He baptized over 500 during one winter. He died suddenly in 1830. His son William was long pastor of South Benson Church, and Hickman Co., KY, was named after his son, Col. Paschal Hickman, who fell in the battle of the river Raisin.

(William Cathcart, *Baptist Encyclopedia*, Vol. 1, p. 521-522)

2. Jeremiah Vardeman

John Vardeman Sr. of Sweden and his wife, Elizabeth, from Wales gave birth to Jeremiah in Wythe County, Virginia. The family moved westward, settling in Kentucky…Jeremiah [at the age of seventeen] made a profession of faith in Jesus Christ as his Savior. However, Jeremiah backslid to the point that his Christian friends gave up hope of his restoration. Jeremiah's mother continued to pray, and he repented, becoming one of God's most useful itinerant preachers and pastors in Kentucky…Jeremiah's ministry was fruitful, causing one of his contemporaries to report that he had probably "baptized more Christian professors than any [other] man in the United States." His baptisms were estimated at "not less than 8,000."

(Cummins/Thompson, *This Day in Baptist History, Vol. 2*, p. 66)

In the spring of 1820, Jeremiah Vardeman came to Nashville, Tennessee, to preach the Gospel. There were all but three Baptist people who lived in Nashville…Under Vardeman a large number of people were saved and baptized and the Baptist church of Nashville was organized on July 22, 1820…By the first of October, the church had 150 members and began building a meeting house.

(Jeremiah Vardeman, p. 472)

As the fall of 1830 commenced, this faithful traveling prophet vacated the fruitful fields of Tennessee and Kentucky for the needy land of Missouri. Missouri, like all of his other places of service, would prove to be a place of great blessings. Vardeman was personally responsible for birthing several churches in that part of the country.

Samuel Howard Ford, onetime pastor of the East Baptist Church in Louisville, known also for the Repository publication, was close friends with Jeremiah Vardeman. Ford said the following concerning Vardeman's successful western ministry: "His success in the ministry of the Gospel was perhaps unequalled by that of any other minister west of the Allegheny Mountains."

J. Gordan Kingsley stated, "Jeremiah Vardeman, a giant of a man at six feet and three hundred pounds and a giant of a preacher who baptized more than 8,000 people in his lifetime."

3. Mordecai Ham

Mordecai Ham was born on April 2, 1877, on his parent's farm in rural Allen County, KY. Ham was born into an ideal situation for becoming a usable tool for the Lord Jesus Christ.

> He was brought up in a hard working family. He had character and a solid work ethic ingrained into him at an early age. He worked those fields daily, under his preacher's/father's watchful eye. Unbeknownst to his father, someday he would be laboring daily in the fields of God with the same relentless work ethic and grit.

> He was brought up in a godly environment. His mother was a woman of unblemished character. His father was a very effective pastor and church planter. Edward Ham stated that Mordecai's dad "pastored fourteen churches, five of which he helped establish…" and he "baptized 1500."
>
> He was cut from a godly cloth. His grandfather (on his father's side) was a prominent pastor in Kentucky. He pastored the Bethlehem Baptist Church for over 40 years. Spencer said of Mordecai F. Ham, Sr. (his grandfather) "It would be safe to say that more than 2,000 persons have been brought into the churches he served."

Everything was in place for the grooming of young Mordecai. In addition to these benefits, he had the prayers of his parents and others that his "grandfather's prophet's mantle would fall on him" (Edward E. Ham). God answered those prayers and the mantle fell on Mordecai. As Elisha of old got a double portion, Mordecai seemed to have a mysteriously earth-shaking power with God and men! He had thousands saved annually, beginning early in his ministry! In all, almost a third of a million converts were added to the churches all over the South!

Ham's fifty year preaching ministry took him to twenty-two states. He saw multitudes of converts and agitated the devil enough to stir up vehement opposition. It is reported that he held a meeting in

Mt. Zion, KY. The local moonshiners showed up and threw rocks at the preachers, while the leader threatened Ham with a long knife. Ham said, "Put up that knife, you coward... Now I'm going to ask the Lord either to convert you and your crowd or kill you." The bully died the next morning before Ham could get to his bedside. That same day the saw mill blew up and killed three others of the crowd. That night Ham proclaimed that he wanted everything that was stolen to be returned before God killed the rest of the tormentors. Everything was returned. A total of eighty were converted before the meeting's end!

Billy Graham was converted under the preaching of Ham in 1934 and was his most well known convert. (This is not an endorsement of Mr. Graham's ministry.)

It was recorded by Ham's nephew Edward that, "Neither the ruffians, of San Benito, TX, who tried to take the Evangelist out and tar and feather him, nor the liquor crowd of Salisbury, North Carolina, that shouted all one night, 'Hang Ham! Hang Ham!' were able to slow his campaigns in twenty-two states" (Edward E. Ham, *Fifty Years on the Battlefront with Christ*).

Hymn Writers

The question has often been asked, "Were there any good evangelists in history that were Baptists?"

As the reader has seen throughout this book, the answer is an absolute "Yes!" Sadly, there has always been a bias against the "narrow-minded, Bible-thumping Baptists." In addition to this, the author has many times confronted the question, "Were there any great Baptist hymn writers?" As you are about to see, a vast majority of the most doctrinally sound, soul-stirring hymns of the faith were penned and composed by Baptists. Enjoy the following brief biographies.

Philip P. Bliss

P. P. Bliss (as he is affectionately remembered) was born in Rome, Pennsylvania, on July 9, 1838. Like David of old is remembered as the sweet psalmist of Israel, P. P. Bliss was the sweet Baptist hymn writer of the 19th and 20th century Baptist churches. Although he never lived to see his 39th birthday, P. P. Bliss is still arguably the greatest Baptist hymn writer in all of history. Gifted by God and inspired by the truth of God's Word, P. P. Bliss both wrote and composed tremendously doctrinal songs for biblical, Baptist churches.

Similar to Mordecai Ham, Bliss grew up in the home of "praying and singing parents." Bliss was saved at the age of twelve and joined the Cherry Flats Baptist Church in Tioga, Pennsylvania. Philip Bliss was married in 1859. The couple moved to Chicago in 1865.

> One night when he attended a revival meeting in Chicago, his marvelous voice came to the attention of the preacher, D. L. Moody, who at the close of the service hastened to speak to him. Moody related in after years, that the "power of solo singing of Gospel songs at evangelistic meetings dated from that time" (Blanchard, *Stories of Beautiful Hymns,* p. 54).

D. L. Moody encouraged Bliss to enter the field of singing as a career. He conceded and gave it his best. Beginning in 1874, Bliss began to work with Major D. W. Whittle as a soloist and song leader. He also worked with children's ministries and wrote hymns and composed music for others.

> In writing to a friend, P. P. Bliss said, "This singing and talking about the Good News of a present, perfect, free salvation and justification by faith is so popular and attractive, I do not believe I shall ever find time for any else" (Blanchard, *Stories of Beautiful Hymns,* p. 55).

Bliss's ministry and life were cut short in the winter of 1876. On December 29th, Bliss and his wife were returning to Chicago after a Christmas visit with his mother and sister. Near Ashtabula, Ohio the train they were riding plunged off a collapsed bridge and landed on the ground below. Bliss lived, and upon exiting the crushed, burning train, realized his wife was still inside. He returned to free her and they both went home to be with the Lord that day. From that day to this, the "sweet Baptist hymn writer of the 19th and 20th century Baptist churches" has been singing his sweet songs in the presence of the Lord Jesus Christ!

The author had the opportunity to visit the memorial marker of the Ashtabula train disaster. That day will never be forgotten. Forty Baptist men stood upright and bellowed out, "Man of Sorrows, what a name, for the Son of God who came, ruined sinners to reclaim, Hallelujah, what a Saviour!" Not an eye remained dry as we honored the memory of Bliss and longed to be in the presence of our God, where Bliss now sings these words with a glorified tongue.

Interesting Facts about P. P. Bliss
- He lived 38 years, 5 months, and 20 days.
- His songs were never copyrighted.
- He once earned only $9 a month as a cook in a lumber camp.
- He taught music.
- In 1865 he earned $100 a month on tour. Later, it went up to $150.
- Moody solicited him to travel with him. Bliss declined but Ira Sankey went.
- He wrote the following hymns:
  "Jesus Loves Even Me"
  "Hallelujah, What a Saviour!"

"My Redeemer"
"Hallelujah, Tis Done!"
"Hold the Fort"
"Whosoever Will"
"Once for All"
"The Light of the World is Jesus"
"Wonderful Words of Life"
"More Holiness Give Me"
"Almost Persuaded"
"Dare to Be a Daniel"
"Let the Lower Lights Be Burning"

- He composed the music for the following hymns:
  "It is Well with My Soul"
  "I Gave My Life for Thee"

Robert Lowry

Robert Lowry was born in Philadelphia, March 12, 1826. Aside from the ministry of P. P. Bliss, none compares to Lowry in the arena of memorable Baptist hymn writers. He was born again in his youth, and at the age of seventeen he became a member of the First Baptist Church of Philadelphia.

He attended the School at Lewisburg, Pennsylvania (now Bucknell University), and graduated in 1854, valedictorian of his class. In the thirty years between 1854 and 1884, he pastored five different churches in Pennsylvania and New York. He labored to plant the Flat Bush Mission in Brooklyn, N. Y. This work is today the Sixth Avenue Baptist Church.

His dearest passion was preaching the Word of God. He was highly intelligent and had a firm grasp on the doctrines of Christ. His second passion was writing and composing music. It is in the latter area where Lowry made his most well known mark on Baptist history.

Lowry wrote the following hymns:

*"**Christ Arose**"* (Has become a traditional "Resurrection Morning" song in Baptist churches)

*"**Nothing But the Blood of Jesus**"* (Considered a Baptist confession of faith in song)

*"**None But Jesus**"* (Lowry's personal favorite)

*"**Shall We Gather at the River**"*

Lowry composed the music for the following hymns:

*"**We're Marching to Zion**"* (Composed for Isaac Watts)

*"**All the Way My Saviour Leads Me**"* (Composed for Fanny Crosby)

*"**I Need Thee Every Hour**"* (Composed for Annie Hawks, a church member)

"Follow On" (Composed for William O. Cushing)
"Something For Thee" (Composed for Sylvanus D. Phelps, the author's personal all-time favorite hymn)

Robert Lowry

On Phelps' 70th birthday, Lowry wrote him the following: "It is worth living seventy years even if nothing comes of it but one such hymn as:

> *Savior! Thy dying love*
> *Thou gavest me;*
> *Nor should I aught withhold,*
> *Dear Lord, from thee.*

Happy is the man who can produce one song which the world will keep on singing after the author shall have passed away. May the tuneful harp preserve its strings for many a long year yet, and the last note reach us only when it is time for the singer to take his place in the heavenly choir" (Robert Lowry).

Other Baptist Hymn Writers
William Doane

Doane was a gifted composer of music for hymns. He composed the music for the following:

> *"Take the Name of Jesus With You"*
> *"Pass Me Not"*
> *"I Am Thine, O Lord"*
> *"Tell Me the Old, Old Story"*
> *"Tis the Blessed Hour of Prayer"*
> *"To God Be the Glory"*
> *"To the Work"*
> *"Rescue the Perishing"*
> *"Will Jesus Find Us Watching"*
> *"Saviour, More Than Life to Me"*
> *"Near the Cross"*
> *"More Love to Thee, O Christ"*

The vast majority of Doane's music was composed for Fanny J. Crosby.

Lesson Ten

William Bradbury

Like Doane, Bradbury's gift was in music composition. Bradbury composed music for the following songs:

> *"Sweet Hour of Prayer"*
> *"Just As I Am"*
> *"Saviour, Like a Shepherd Lead Us"*
> *"Holy Bible, Book Divine"*
> *"Even Me"*
> *"Depth of Mercy"*
> *"There Is No Name So Sweet On Earth"*
> *"Tis Midnight-And On Olive's Brow"*

In addition to this, he is responsible for composing the music for what is arguably the most sung Christian song since its birth, "Jesus Loves Me."

Honorable Mention

Samuel Stennett
> *"Majestic Sweetness Sits Enthroned"*
> *"On Jordan's Stormy Banks"*

Peter Billhorn
> *"Sweet Peace, the Gift of God's Love"*
> *"I Will Sing the Wondrous Story"*

Joseph Gilmore
> **"He Leadeth Me"**

Edward Mote
> **"The Solid Rock"**

Robert Robinson
> **"Come Thou Fount"**

Annie Hawks
> **"I Need Thee Every Hour"**

Samuel Francis Smith
> **"My Country, Tis of Thee"**
> **"The Morning Light Is Breaking"**

Sivilla D. Martin
> **"God Will Take Care of You"**
> **"His Eye Is on the Sparrow"**

John Rippon
> **"How Firm a Foundation"**
> **"All Hail the Power"**

Review Questions

1. It would be easy to write volumes on the subject of godly "second _____."

Lesson Ten

2. Thousands of _____ _____ could be brought to light if the records were available.

3. William Hickman was born in the state of _____.

4. Hickman baptized more than _____ during one winter.

5. One of Vardeman's contemporaries said he probably "baptized more _____ _____ than any [other] man in the United States."

6. Under Vardeman a large number of people were saved and baptized and the Baptist church of _____ was organized on July 22, 1820.

7. By the first of October, the church had _____ members and began building a _____ _____.

8. As the fall of 1830 commenced, Vardeman vacated the fruitful fields of Tennessee and Kentucky for the needy land of _____.

9. J. Gordan Kingsley stated, "Jeremiah Vardeman, a giant of a man of six feet and _____ pounds and a giant of a preacher who baptized more than _____ people in his lifetime."

10. Mordecai Ham's father baptized _____ people.

11. Mordecai Ham's grandfather brought _____ people into the churches.

12. Mordecai had the prayers of his parents and many others that his "grandfather's prophet's mantle would fall _____ _____."

13. In all, almost a third of__ _____ converts were added to the churches all over the South under Ham's ministry.

14. _____ _____ was converted under the preaching of Ham in 1934 and was his most well known convert.

15. Although he never lived to see his 39th birthday, P. P. Bliss was still arguably the greatest Baptist _____ _____ in all of history.

Lesson Ten

16. P. P. Bliss both wrote and composed tremendously _____ songs for biblical, _____ churches.

17. ____ ____ _____ encouraged Bliss to enter the field of singing as a career.

18. Bliss and his wife were killed near _____, Ohio.

19. Bliss's songs were never _____.

20. Robert Lowry was born in _____.

21. Lowry pastored _____ different churches in Pennsylvania and New York.

22. Lowry labored to plant the Flat Bush Mission in _____, _____ _____.

23. William _____ was a gifted composer of music for hymns.

24. Like Doane, _____'s gift was in music composition.

25. Bradbury is responsible for composing the music for what is arguably the most sung Christian song since its birth, "_____ _____ _____."

Lesson Eleven

Southern Baptist Convention/ Independent Baptists

And the contention was so sharp between them, that they departed asunder one from the other…
Acts 15:39a

In 1845 a convention of several key Baptists met in Augusta, Georgia, resulting in the creation of the Southern Baptist Convention. When the Southern Baptist Convention began, an era of independence among Baptist churches ended. This schism has proven to be the largest division among Baptists in American history to this day. The split ultimately had diverse effects. The negative effects can be clearly seen from the viewpoint of the 21st century, separated, independent Baptist. The Convention that was created that day in Georgia, so many years ago, has in the last few decades taken marked steps to the left both theologically and practically. It truly is sad to see so many churches and individuals rally under the name of Baptist, who have embraced hyper-Calvinism, modern Bibles, and contemporary trends in their worship services. The personal dress standards which independent Baptists consider normal Christian living, the average Southern Baptist today considers extreme legalism. It would be fair to assume that if every Southern Baptist church had remained independent and the convention wasn't dictating the liberal standard they now maintain, many of these churches could very well be strong, independent Baptist churches that are pleasing to God. In that sense, America would probably be a better place, had the Baptists never split in 1845. The ecclesiastical control that the SBC wields over its churches has been their downfall.

Years later, when the division was final, a new organization arose in the North called the American Baptist Missionary Union. Other divisions among Baptists in both the North and the South would produce the American Baptist Association (ABA), Northern Baptist Convention (NBC), Conservative Baptist Association (CBA), the General Association of Regular Baptist Churches (GARBC), and the Baptist Bible Fellowship International (BBFI) among others. The "Fundamentalist Movement" would eventually arise as a reaction to German rationalism and modernism among the Protestants. Many Baptists became a part of the Fundamentalist Movement; some did not. The author holds to the view that the separated, independent, Baptist churches that hold to the infallibility of the King

James Bible are the one type of church that through all the splits and splinters still most clearly reflect the churches in the New Testament. The Independent Baptist churches are in the lineage of true, scriptural churches.

This lesson is intended to take the reader through the specifics of these divisions. The key Baptists who were involved in these various groups will be given mention. Ultimately, the student of Baptist history, upon studying this lesson, should know where the independent Baptist movement came from, how it started, and why they are an independent Baptist. History has proven that people who don't know where they came from, and cannot tell you why they are what they are, will rarely have the conviction to stand for what they are.

The Triennial Convention – Unity for the Sake of Missions

When missionary Adoniram Judson was convinced of Baptist principles and was subsequently dropped by the Congregationalists, the need became apparent for an agency to support his work. Although we believe the local church is biblically responsible and completely capable of supporting missionaries in such endeavors, the Baptists at that time saw it differently. In May of 1814, the General Missionary Convention of the Baptist Denomination in the United States of America for Foreign Missions was founded. It was to meet every three years and was therefore known by the shorter name of Triennial Convention. Luther Rice was elected to raise funds for the work by representing the need to churches and associations. Although there have been a good many schisms among the Baptists through the years, in the early 1800s there was a spirit of unity and cooperation among many Baptists. There has, among certain Baptists in America, always been a belief that there should be some sort of centralized authority structure to a greater or lesser degree. W. W. Barnes wrote about this in his book simply titled, *The Southern Baptist Convention*. Consider this helpful discussion:

> "...denominational consciousness was still prominent. There were certain ideas embodied in the ecclesiology of the Baptists...that determined the thinking then and has continued to the present to determine trends in Southern Baptist life. The centralized thinking in ecclesiology in those areas derived from three sources:
>
> *The Philadelphia Confession of Faith,* used widely among the churches of the South, carries the conception of the general, invisible church (a conception brought over from the Westminister Confession, to which the Philadelphia one goes back in origin), as well as of the particular church.

LESSON ELEVEN

Article 26 (#1)

The catholick or universal church, which...may be invisible, consists of the whole number of the Elect that have been, are, or shall be gathered into one under Christ.

The original Baptist life, finding expression in Virginia and North Carolina, came from the General Baptists in England. Although the General Baptists were Arminian in theology, in opposition to the Calvinism of the Philadelphia Confession, they held to a centralized ecclesiology in agreement with the fundamental spiritual idea of the Philadelphia. Their General Assembly exemplified externally the invisible church idea of the Philadelphia Confession.

The General Baptist Creed of 1678 (England) states:

Article #39

"General councils, or assemblies, consisting of Bishops, Elders, and Brethren, of the several churches of Christ, and being legally convened, and met together out of all the churches and the churches appearing there by their representatives, make but one church, and have lawful right, and suffrage in this general meeting, or assembly, to act in the best means under heaven to preserve unity, [and] to prevent heresy..."

The great Baptist progress south of the Potomac began after 1750 with the coming of the Separate Baptists from New England. These were converts from Congregationalism and Presbyterianism during the

Great Awakening. Shubael Stearns and Daniel Marshall, the principal leaders, were never wholly freed from the ideas of ecclesiology they inherited from the past. The Sandy Creek Association was the large body that included all Separate Baptists until 1771. That association functioned as an ecclesiastical body, examining and baptizing candidates, examining and ordaining ministers.

As a result of these three inheritances, Baptist leaders south of Philadelphia, as a rule, favored a national denominational organization more than did the leaders north of Philadelphia.

(W. W. Barnes, *The Southern Baptist Convention*)

Division Inevitable

It is evident, then, that there were many factors influencing Baptists to be unified. However, that desired unity may have been wishful thinking from the very beginning. The pride that attempts to take up residence in every man's heart was at work from the earliest of days in the colonies. Barnes bears this fact out in the introduction to the before mentioned book.

From Colonial times there were rivalries and jealousies between the Northern and Southern colonies. The big problem of the revolutionary leaders was to secure co-operation among the colonies, the allegiance of each of which had been directly to the

Crown of England. After Yorktown and the achievement of political independence, the problem was to hold the thirteen independent states together. The great distances, the poor roads, the lack of facilities of travel, and other means of communication, hindered unity of thinking and acting. In formulating the Constitution for the basis of federal union, the jealousies between the Northern and Southern sections, between the large and small states, almost wrecked the effort.

These struggles culminated in the War Between the States.

The same conditions that hindered unity of thinking and acting in secular life affected the Baptist groups in different parts of the land. In addition, varying emphases in doctrine, in ecclesiology, in church polity were brought from Europe, and comparable differences developed among the various groups in this country. Some of these differences entered into the separation between Baptists of the South and the North in 1845.

Barriers to Unity

The disagreements among the Northern and Southern Baptists were there, brewing under the surface, for many years prior to 1845. And yet, in spite of all of the age-old bad blood between these two factions, when the true obstacles to unity began to surface, they were much more pronounced! There were basically two reasons for the division which was about to transpire. The first was a minor factor, and the second was the main reason for the split.

The Supposed Neglect of the Southern Colonies

The General Convention was already in place to promote foreign missions. In 1832 the American Baptist Home Mission Society was formed. Based in New York, its motto was "North America for Christ." The vast majority of its missionaries came from the North and were sent to fields in the North. From its inception, the society was accused of taking Southern money and using it primarily to win the North for Christ. At the same time, it was also accused of neglecting the souls in the South. Consider this scathing article which appeared in a Nashville based Christian newspaper in 1835:

> It appears from the last report of the Executive Committee of the American Baptist Home Mission Society that they have not a single missionary in all Kentucky, Alabama, Louisiana and Florida, and that they partially or entirely sustain one missionary in Mississippi, three in Tennessee and three in Arkansas, making in all seven missionaries for these six states and one Territory... only one missionary to every 428,581 souls, while in the state of Michigan,...

> they have sixteen missionaries...one missionary to every 4,000 souls...supplied. Are they more needy? Are they more destitute? Why are these states (Illinois and Indiana) so liberally supplied? They are more liberally supplied because of Northern contributions, and because Northern preachers refuse to come to the South...It is, therefore, apparent, that the only way to produce effort in the South must be brought about by the formation of a Southern Baptist Home Mission Society.

In 1844, one year before the Southern Baptist Convention was formed, the following article appeared in the *Religious Herald:*

> ...Our contributions have been generally expended in the ...West, Michigan, Indiana, Ohio, Illinois, and the territories of Iowa and Wisconsin. A few missionaries have been sent to Missouri, a still smaller number to Arkansas and Texas. ...Meanwhile the South and Southwestern new states, equally destitute, have been measurably overlooked.

There is disagreement as to whether these injustices were actual or simply perceived. Some historians claim it was difficult to get missionaries to go south, even when the mission society desired to send them. Whether or not this is the case is uncertain; we do know that the need in the North was far greater than in the South. The North had no Separate Baptist revival, and there were far less churches in the regions that the Convention was focused on. Iowa, for example, did not have a single Baptist church until 1834! The anger over missions was likely being fueled by the anger over the true issue of disagreement, slavery.

Slavery

The biggest reason for the South to "secede" from the General Missionary Convention centered on the issue of slavery. While missionary/statesman Dr. J. M. Peck and others tried to downplay the schism over slavery and hold the Baptists together, a great parting of ways was about to take place.

In 1844, the…

> "Board of the General Missionary Convention of the Baptist Denomination located in Boston passed a resolution stating they could no longer approve a slaveholder to be a missionary. This inevitable decision was a great grief and offense to the South" (Beller).

Barnes said,
> "But abolitionists were active and persistent. Churches and associations were won, first to condemnation of slavery and then to non-fellowship with those who had any sort of connection with slavery."

Lesson Eleven

The Convention is Born

Emotions ran high and the stage was set for a separation between the Northern and Southern Baptists. In an editorial review of the thirteenth annual report of the Home Missions Society—nine Southern states reporting—it said:

> "The South will not only lose nothing by being thrust out from the Northern Society; but it also proves that the domestic missions of the South can be better sustained in our separate existence..."

Complaints from the South only multiplied and by 1844 the Baptists in the South were nearly unanimous in support of a separation. Dr. R. B. C. Howell of Nashville, representing the General Association of Tennessee,

> "recognized that separation from the Board must come for three reasons: The Board had done violence to the Word of God, had violated the constitution of the General Convention, and had reversed the judgment of the whole church as expressed in the last session of the Convention" (Barnes).

After much discussion, including varied opinions and deliberations, the Southern Baptist Convention was organized with the aid of W. B. Johnson. Upon the adoption of the constitution, Dr. J. B.

Jeter submitted the following:

> Resolved, That the individuals, churches and other bodies, approving the Constitution of the Southern Baptist Convention, adopted by this body, be recommended to meet, according to its provisions, for organization, by members of delegates,… in Richmond, VA. : And that this Convention now proceed to the election of Officers and Boards of Managers, to continue in office until said meeting.

Upon this decision, the Southern Baptist Convention was born!

The SBC had well over 35,000 churches in 2009. Ironically, today (2010), Southern Baptist churches can be found as far north as Wisconsin and Michigan. These were two of the states that the Southern churches were agitated with, because they supposedly received too much mission support. At the time the Convention was formed, it would have been impossible to find a Southern Baptist Church in the North. The SBC was started for Baptist churches in anti-abolitionist states and for the support of missionaries to the South. Because of the sentiment of the day over slavery, rights, and missions, the Baptist churches in the South were almost entirely brought under the umbrella of the SBC. Very few remained independent of the Convention.

The North and South after the Split

"The Triennial Convention of the Baptists was dissolved" (Beller). In the North, very few churches remained unaffiliated.

The North/NBC

1. The Northern Baptist Convention (NBC) was founded in 1907.
2. In 1923 the Baptist Bible Union (BBU) was formed by a conservative group of men within the NBC. In 1932 the BBU separated from the Northern Baptist Convention. At this time, the BBU formed the General Association of Regular Baptist Churches (GARBC).
3. In 1951 another group within the Northern Baptist Convention, opposed to the compromise, set out to form a more biblical group called the Conservative Baptist Fellowship. The CBF, in 1967, renamed itself as the Fundamental Baptist Fellowship.

The GARBC and FBF are now acceptant of the corrupt, modern Bible versions and have been negatively influenced by reformed theology (Calvinism).

The NBC, through continued compromise, has become a shame and reproach to the Lord Jesus Christ. In 1950 the convention changed its name to the American Baptist Convention. In 1972 the American Baptist Convention changed its name to the American Baptist Churches in the USA (ABC). Women preachers, rock music, and many other doctrinal errors and sins are earmarks of this movement!

The ABC is not to be confused with the ABA, which was a split from the Southern Baptist Convention and is still much more conservative than the ABC in both doctrine and practice.

The South/SBC

1. The Southern Baptist Convention had a split in 1905, and the ABA (American Baptist Association) was started under the leadership of Ben M. Bogard. This split was over the support of missions and ecclesiology. The ABA developed from churches that wanted to maintain a strong position on the ordinances and other local church issues, as well as the scriptural support of missions. The SBC was moving away from these historic positions and practices.

2. The Baptist Missionary Association (BMA) formed in 1950 as a split off of the ABA.

3. In the early 1900's there arose great controversy over the "fundamentals" of the faith. A bold preacher from Texas named J. Frank Norris led in the opposition to those denying the "fun-

damentals" within the SBC. This split from the SBC would produce the World Baptist Fellowship (WBF).

4. The Baptist Bible Fellowship International (BBFI) split from the WBF in 1950 under the leadership of G. B. Vick, and was a greatly used movement. John Rawlings, Noel Smith, and Art Wilson were strong leaders in the BBFI for many years.

The Convention Veers Left

By the early 1920s it became evident that the Southern Baptist Convention was headed to the left on many issues. Separation, both ecclesiastically and personally, has been a major problem in the Convention since then. Doctrinal issues have also remained a thorn in the flesh of the SBC. When gifted men, with the strength to do something about it, came along, the independent Baptist movement started. The early leaders of the independent Baptists were mostly men who separated from the SBC. We'll discuss that shortly, but for now, we need to consider the creation of Fundamentalism.

Fundamentalism

A full discussion concerning Fundamentalism was a part of *Volume 1* of this curriculum. At this juncture we will simply restate that "Baptists throughout the ages held to certain distinctives that caused them to hold to a rigid separation from error, at any cost. In the early 1900s the Evangelical Alliance was fighting the battle of German rationalism in their schools. These non-Baptist, Protestant schools were threatened to the point of total apostasy through this heresy. When the Evangelical Alliance finally took a stand on certain, basic Christian doctrines, many Baptists in their day applauded them. What happened next was an event that would hurt Baptists in many ways. The Evangelical Alliance produced the Fundamentalist Movement. The Term "Fundamentalism" began to be used more and more frequently as a series of books entitled *"The Fundamentals: A Testimony to the Truth"* were written and circulated starting in 1915. In 1919 W. B. Riley started the World Christian Fundamentals Association. Everyone who rejected German rationalism and adhered to certain, basic Bible doctrines was welcomed in the club. Sadly, some Baptists inadvertently turned their backs on ecclesiastical separation and 1900 years of glorious Baptist history, and unwisely joined the ranks of Fundamentalism. Remember that most of these fundamentalist churches were the daughters of Rome, having as their origin and alleged authority, the Protestant Reformation" (Some of this information appeared in *Baptist Heritage Course, Vol. 1 – The Ancient Church*, Ted Alexander).

As time progressed and compromise among the various denominations reappeared, the Baptists became the sole beacon of Fundamentalism. Methodism, Presbyterianism, Lutheranism, and the other participants in the Fundamentalist Movement have long since revealed themselves as apostates. This revelation was inevitable, as the reformers are the corrupt fruit of the poisonous tree of Roman Catholicism. Truly, "all of Rome's babies went back to Mama."

Independent Baptists

Before the Southern Baptist Convention began, all Baptists were independent. There were associations, but there was not a strong power structure as would be seen in the Southern Baptist Convention. As the years went by, the SBC took a progressive path to the left of center. Evolution found a place in SBC schools, as well as teaching which rejected premillenialism. There were problems with the Convention's view of missions and who it supported. These problems, in addition to the separation issues before mentioned, would not be tolerated by all. And as a result of this, several Baptist ministers "pulled out" of the Southern Baptist Convention. The floodtide began with Dr. J. Frank Norris. He left the Convention and started a college in Ft. Worth, Texas. Next, men like Dr. Lee Roberson, Dr. Dallas Billington,

John R. Rice, Lester Roloff, John Rawlings, and G. B. Vick departed from the Convention. Jack Hyles, Lee Roberson, and Harold Sightler became high profile leaders, pastoring large independent Baptist works. These charismatic leaders soon developed a large following, and the 20th century Independent Fundamental Baptist Movement was created. This is still a popular movement in 2010. The complete assessment of this movement may be the subject of a future manuscript. There have been many positive results of the labors of the Independent Fundamental Baptists in America. There have also been negative ramifications of mixing the Baptist faith with Fundamentalism. Protestant doctrine and practice crept in among Baptists through the door of Fundamentalism. Although we do not doubt the motives of the early Fundamental Baptist leaders, not everything they did was by the Book.

Not all independent Baptists from 1940 through 1970 came out of the Convention; in fact, many were independent all along. Other leaders of the independent Baptist movement of the previous 75 years were from the North. Some of these had associational ties prior to their being swept into the independent Baptist movement, and some had no previous ties.

Dr. James Beller, in his *Baptist Workbook*, stated the following as the "Seven great influences on the independent, fundamental Baptists of the twentieth century:"

- The Baptist Bible Fellowship. J. Frank Norris and Beauchamp Vick
- The General Association of Regular Baptists. Dr. Bob Ketchem
- The Conservative Baptist movement. Dr. Myron Cedarholm
- The Southwide Baptist Fellowship. Dr. Harold Sightler and Dr. Lee Roberson
- The Sword of the Lord influence. Dr. John Rice
- The Pastor School influence. Dr. Jack Hyles
- The Christian School movement

Biblical Baptists

The author realizes that not everyone who is an independent Baptist today wants to be affiliated with a "movement." Many are desirous to be known as Independent Baptists and avoid the term "Fundamentalist." This position is consistent with that of the author. It is imperative to remember that before the SBC and before Fundamentalism, there were old-fashioned, independent, Baptist churches that were consistent with the New Testament churches in the Word of God. While we are thankful for the good done by Independent Fundamental Baptists, we hope that all Baptists see the problems with our attachment to Fundamentalism and once again strive to be pure in our affiliations, identification, doctrine, and practice. The author identifies himself simply as a Bible-believing, independent Baptist!

Review Questions

1. The dress standards that independent Baptists consider normal, the average Southern Baptist today considers _____ _____.

2. America would probably be a better place had the Baptists never _____ in 1845.

3. The student of Baptist history should know where the independent Baptist movement _____ _____, how it started, and why they are an independent Baptist.

4. People who don't know where they came from and cannot tell you why they are what they are, will rarely have the _____ to _____ for what they are.

5. When _____ Judson was convinced of Baptist principles, he was subsequently

Lesson Eleven

dropped by the _____.

6. Luther _____ was elected to raise funds for the _____ Convention.

7. There has, among certain Baptists in America, always been a belief that there should be some sort of _____ _____ structure.

8. "Baptist leaders south of Philadelphia favored a national _____ _____ more than did the leaders north of Philadelphia."

9. "From Colonial times there were rivalries and jealousies between the _____ and _____ colonies."

10. The General Convention was accused of neglecting the souls in the _____.

11. The North and South split mainly over the issue of _____.

12. The SBC was born in the year _____.

13. The SBC had a substantial split in _____,

and the ABA was formed. This split was over the support of missions and _____.

14. The General Association of Regular Baptists (GARBC) was created in 1932 by the _____ _____ Union.

15. The CBF renamed itself as the _____ _____ _____.

16. The Northern Baptist Convention changed its name to the _____ _____ _____.

17. The early leaders of the _____ Baptists were mostly men who separated from the SBC.

18. As time progressed and compromise among the various denominations reappeared, the _____ became the sole beacon of Fundamentalism.

19. It is imperative to remember that before the SBC and before Fundamentalism, there were old-fashioned independent Baptist churches that were consistent with the _____

Lesson Eleven

_____ churches in the Word of God.

20. We hope that all Baptists see the problems with our attachment to Fundamentalism and once again strive to be pure in our _____, _____, _____, and _____.

Lesson Twelve

Baptists in the 21st Century

> Wherefore seeing we also are compassed about with so great a cloud of witnesses, let us lay aside every weight, and the sin which doth so easily beset *us*, and let us run with patience the race that is set before us, Looking unto Jesus…
> **Hebrews 12:1-2a**

Dear friend, you are about to tackle the final lesson in the two volume study on Baptist heritage. If you started with book one (The Ancient Church), this is your 24th lesson. Do not make the mistake of thinking that this last lesson is not a necessary lesson; on the contrary, it is the most important and needed of all of the lessons. This lesson teaches the student to apply everything he has studied in Baptist history. If Baptist history is worth examining at all, it is because it leaves the reader changed. Examining history allows the student to learn from the mistakes of others. It also allows for a person to grow from seeing the successes and triumphs of others. Over the years, the author has made it a habit to quiz older men of God. They have told me of wisdom they have learned over lifetime ministries.

The author has tried to apply these lessons learned to his own ministry. Why should we suffer from the same mistakes others have made? In this sense, history becomes our friend and helps guide us in the present.

One of the elements that make Bible preaching good Bible preaching is whether or not the preacher applies the truth to the listener's lives. Whether he "drives the truth home" or not can make or break a message. The same principle stands true in studying history. If we apply the lessons we have learned from Baptist history, we will be better for it. The wisdom we learn from the study of how the scriptural churches acted in the past is so valuable because it can be obtained in no other way than by a diligent study of the historical record. If we do not learn from the errors of previous generations, we are wasting a valuable opportunity to do better for the Lord. The Old Testament record of the rebellious and disobedient nation of Israel was given to us to be "profitable" (2 Timothy 3:16). The Lord expects us to learn from the sins and failures of God's people in the past. He does not want us to repeat the same sins of our spiritual forefathers. In like manner, as we honor our Baptist Christian forebears, we must be diligent not to let their mistakes go unnoticed. Let us examine their doctrine and learn from it! Let us look at their character and scrutinize it to the end that we might be a people of godly character. Let us see their practice; then comparing it with the Scriptures, we should retain that which is true to God's Word and discard the rest. We must not let their work and sacrifice be in vain. Above all, may we not behold our history as one that beholdeth his face in a glass then walks away unchanged (James, Ch. 1). We can and we must learn the wisdom God has for us through the study of our Baptist heritage. Otherwise, God will not find us guiltless!

Learning from History

This section will deal with several lessons that must be learned from the study of Baptist history. Although this present study book covers American Baptist history, we will momentarily reach back into the content covered in the first book. Looking diligently at the whole of history, from apostolic times to the present, the most pressing lessons we must glean are as follows:

Liberty

As one studies the Baptists, from the time of John, Christ, and the apostles, it becomes glaringly evident that there has always been a struggle for liberty of conscience. Liberty has had its enemies in every generation. In New Testament times, we see the struggle as John was beheaded, Christ was crucified, and the apostles suffered great persecutions. Steven and Paul suffered greatly. The religious crowd hated Steven so much that they bit him and stoned him.

The emperor Diocletian, along with other Roman governmental leaders, made the 2nd and 3rd centuries a horrible time of persecution. Rome, under the pagan deities, was not a friend to liberty. Rome's emperor Constantine married state and church in A. D. 313 and that move proved to be an even greater swipe at the face of liberty. The Roman Catholic (universal) institution persecuted the ancient Baptists all over Europe for over a thousand years.

It is interesting to note that all of the symbols used by the Waldenses represented the struggle for liberty. The flower wrapped in a thorny vine with the inscription, "struggling and freeing oneself," being the most striking example.

Then came the Reformation and the dawn of a new day. Truly the religious landscape in Europe changed, but not in favor of the Baptists. The Protestant offspring (Reformers) of the Roman Catholic institution viewed liberty as a threat, as their mother Rome had for many centuries.

In the early 1600s history unfolded on the shores of a new land, what is called today, the Land of Liberty. This however was not the case in the beginning. When our forebears began practicing liberty in this land, they were shocked to see "New England becoming old." Early America saw a transplant of state-sponsored religion. The "state-church" is the greatest enemy liberty has ever seen. Baptists throughout the entire colonial period suffered many atrocities because of their insistence of liberty.

We have already discussed the fact that this struggle for liberty finally produced a bill of individual rights as amendments to our Constitution.

The Baptists are one of the only groups of people who have understood liberty. May we suggest three distinct views concerning liberty throughout the ages?

The Heathen View

This view comes from those lost in sin. They are doing the works of their father the Devil. They embrace pagan gods or worship the flesh. In history, those holding this view persecuted any who denied the pagan deities or rejected the fleshly principle of their civil government. There was no liberty of conscience, therefore there was no liberty.

The Catholic or Reformed View

This viewpoint was introduced by Augustine and handed to the Catholic institution as a viable theology. Augustine's view was that the "universal church" was the spiritual city of God on earth. This fact gave them the right, or so they believed, to persecute all dissenters with death, if necessary. This was also the view of Luther, Calvin, Zwingli, and Knox. The reformed groups reject Roman Catholicism in part, but maintain its view of civil government. The Catholic Reformed are on a "mission from God" to dominate the world and set up the kingdom of God for Him. This requires that the power of the state uphold the doctrine of the "universal church."

The Biblical Baptist Worldview

"Liberty of conscience" for everyone! This was the view of the vast majority of our Baptist forefathers. This viewpoint, being embraced by the Baptists, won the right to worship freely for all! The Baptist worldview is one in which all men have a God-given right to search the Scriptures for themselves and do with the Christ of the Bible what they choose. They might accept Him, and they might reject Him; but that is the freewill choice of every man, as granted by God Himself. Baptists therefore have never persecuted anyone in order to make them join our "church." Baptists realize that men must have the liberty to reject Christ, if there is to be any hope that some will truly accept Him! The Baptist worldview is one in which there can be absolutely no church/state entanglement whatsoever.

Lesson Twelve

This entanglement has been proven to be detrimental to liberty, as those who are in charge always attempt to control the hearts and minds of men.

*The lesson we must learn from all of this is quite simple. As our Baptist forefathers rejected the heathen worldview, so do we reject it. Sadly, however, many Baptists today have been lured into embracing the reformed worldview. Our Baptist forebears would never have done the things many Baptists do today. For example, many Baptists today have incorporated their churches, thereby stepping into an unnecessary entanglement with the state. It is nearly impossible to break the yoke of incorporation. If a church chooses to do so, all properties must be donated to another non-profit organization. Once incorporated, the state holds great sway if a church wants out. Is Christ the head of the church if you cannot break the yoke without obeying the state's outlandish demand of relinquishing all of your property? Incorporation could prove to be the Baptists' "Trojan Horse!" Can you imagine the imprisoned colonial preachers yoking up with the state? In addition, some Baptists today have bought the lie that there "can be no separation of church and state." On the contrary, there absolutely must be a separation; otherwise, the state will begin to control the churches. If the average "reformed" Baptist of today would have been alive during the state-church persecutions that happened in the colonies, they would have been abhorred by the brethren! How would you explain that the separation of church and state is a "myth" to a Baptist preacher who was sitting in jail suffering at the hands of a state-church? Any entanglement of church and state is a potential threat to the liberty we hold so dear.

Many Baptists today are proud of spending taxpayer's money on "faith based initiatives." And yet if it were Muslim mosques that were getting taxpayer's money, Baptists would be irate. There would be concern that the Muslims were trying to take over. Why can we see that as wrong, but when there is a threat of Christians taking over, many applaud. What is absolutely urgent to understand is that every state-church that ever existed has persecuted dissenters. A state-church is a kind of hybrid monster that God never intended to exist! This is true whether the Catholics rule, the reformed Catholics rule, or even if the Baptists were in control. Once liberty would be lost to a state-church of any kind, it would be nearly impossible to restore.

It took about 1800 years for liberty to be established as it has been in America. We must fight to maintain it, especially from its oldest and worst enemy—an established church.

Questions to ponder:
- Can a reformed politician defend liberty properly?
- Should Baptists use curriculum that teaches history and Bible from a reformed viewpoint?

While many of these issues may not seem that important, they are all stepping stones on the pathway to a monstrous state-church! The influence Baptists have on civil government must be the kind of influence that transpires when men that fully understand liberty are elected to office. We must seek out, promote, and vote for those candidates, even if it means losing some elections. We will all give an account to God for our voting record. Vote for the candidates that truly want to uphold the Constitution and Bill of Rights and that embrace true liberty for all. These biblical Baptist principles are ones that we will never have to apologize to God for embracing.

Doctrine

Another lesson we should learn from the Baptists of bygone years is a lesson concerning doctrine. As we look at history, there are some things that stand out.

1. Baptists have always been very sober minded

and unwilling to bend in their doctrine.

2. Baptists have always been strong protectors of the ordinances of the local church.

3. Baptists have always believed in the local, visible church as opposed to the Catholic, invisible, universal church.

4. Baptists have always been willing to defend their doctrine when challenged by others.

Since we know that millions of Baptists were willing to die over the doctrine of baptism alone, then we as Baptists cannot help but stand firmly against doctrinal compromise in our day. Anything else would be disobedience to God, disrespect to our forefathers, and a disservice to our children!

- Look up I Timothy 4:16. What two parties did Paul tell Timothy would be saved by sound doctrine?
- Look up I Corinthians 11:2. How did Paul say the ordinances should be kept?
- Look up II John 1:8-11. If Baptist Christians are sympathetic and friendly toward those holding false doctrine, what do we become?

Godly Character

Yet another lesson that can be gleaned from Baptist history is a lesson in character. This lesson is one that is desperately needed in our day and age. It would be easy, as a staunch Baptist, for the author to relate only the history that paints the Baptists as a people of great character. The only barrier to trying to portray Baptist history in such a way is that it is not necessary. As the author looks long and hard at 2,000 years of Baptist history, it is abundantly clear that character did abound in and among the Baptists.

Alexis Muston recorded the following excerpt in his Waldensian history entitled *Israel of the Alps*:

> The Grand Inquisitor, in virtue of the powers with which he was invested, now required the aid of the military to execute his commission. Two companies of soldiers were placed at his disposal. He sent them into the woods of St. Xist to bring back the fugitives; but scarcely had they discovered their retreat, when they fell upon them, crying, "Kill! Kill!" The unfortunate Vaudois tried to make their escape; the soldiers pursued them in all directions, as if they were engaged in the destruction of wild beasts. At last some of the fugitives gathered upon a mountain, and demanded a parley. The captain of the soldiers advanced. "Spare us!" they exclaimed, "spare us! What harm have we done you? Have pity on our wives and children! Have we not been here for centuries, without having given any cause of complaint? Are we not loyal subjects, industrious labourers, and peaceable well-doing people?"
>
> "You are devils, transformed into angels of light, to seduce the simple," was the reply, "but the Holy Of-

fice has unmasked your errors." "Well, then," said they, "if we may not be permitted to profess the faith of our forefathers in peace, in these countries which we have rendered fertile, we offer to leave them, and to retire into another country."

"You will go to sow there the poison of your heresy. No mercy for the rebels!" cried he. And giving the order for his troops to attack them, he advanced with his men amongst the rocks where the Vaudois had sheltered themselves (*Israel of the Alps*, p. 87).

In this quote we see the Waldenses, as they pled for their lives, inadvertently recording for us their character and work ethic. This is not their intention, to brag, as it were. They only point to their character as a good reason for the Romanists not to slaughter them. The historical record of the godly character of the Baptists is well documented in every century and among all the various Baptist groups.

In the 7th and 8th centuries the Paulicians were Baptist Christians of great character. Their ministers were of such character that when being ordained to the ministry, it was by taking the following oath: "I take on myself scourging, imprisonments, tortures, reproaches, crosses, blows, tribulation and all temptations of the world" (Broadbent).

The Bogomils of the 8th and 9th centuries were "in favor of a very simple brand of Christianity" and were known as "the friends of God." The Paterines of the 11th century were "know to have been people who emphasized personal separation. They were decent in their deportment, modest in their dress and discourse, and their morals were irreproachable" (Ted Alexander, "Baptist Heritage Conf. Syllabus," p. 23 and compiled from numerous sources).

Today we hear stories of Baptist ministers quitting the ministry, getting caught in adultery, fleecing the sheep, and covering sin for one another. We often hear the world say that they are not interested in "organized religion" because of all the hypocrites. This charge is not completely baseless. What we need today is to look to our forebears, examine their manner of life, and beg God for a good dose of that old-fashioned character that used to describe the Baptists.

Evangelism/Church Planting

The Baptists have always been a people of action. The Bible they believe calls them to such action. Our Baptist forebears were doers and not hearers only. They were not willing to sit idly by while the world died and went to hell! Many Baptists today are slumping over in lethargy. Hyper-calvinism, unconcern, and just pure laziness are killing us. We would do well to examine the record of Baptists with their labors and learn from them. When one considers the numbers of Baptist martyrs through the ages, a question arises. If there were tens of millions of martyrs in the 2,000 years of church history, then how did the churches still flourish? If the great whore is truly drunken with the blood of the Baptists as Revelation 17 tells us, how did the Baptists not just live on, but multiply greatly? The answer is that they were involved in serious evangelism.

The Waldensian peddlers went door to door, witnessing under threat of death. Henry of Lousanne, Switzerland, preached in the streets in an attempt to rescue souls and was starved to death in prison because of it. Peter de Bruys preached the Gospel publicly with great power and was burned to death. Arnold of Brescia preached for souls in Rome until a revival coupled with a rebellion broke out. He was crucified and burnt. His ashes were scattered over the Tiber River. Walter Lollard's revival preaching ministry encompassed many miles up and down the Rhine River region. His converts were multitudinous and spilled over into England. The Anabaptist Balthaser Hubmaier was called "the great apostle to the Baptists of Moravia." History records that he had over 6,000 converts in Moravia.

The Separate Baptists of America were one of the most zealous evangelistic bodies in all of history. They preached continually, won souls, and birthed churches. The church planting of the Separate Baptists was so successful that Baptists of today would be foolish to ignore it. Sadly, most Baptists today are either ignorant of the church planting of the Separate Baptists or they know about it but have never let the facts change them.

We would be very wise in our day to use the Separate Baptists as a model for modern day church planting efforts. The reader is hereby challenged to look carefully at the history of the Sandy Creek Baptist Church, Shubal Stearns, and the rest of the Separate Baptists. Ask the Lord how you can personally be involved in promoting church planting today. If we do not learn from the history of the Separate Baptists, we will most likely continue to watch America decline spiritually!

Writing a New Chapter

Dear reader, you are about to complete book 2 and complete your present study of Baptist history. I want to take this time to share with you the burden of my heart. First, let me thank you for your interest in this study. It encourages me to know there are so many Baptists today who want to know their history. Secondly, let me encourage you to continue your study. We have covered nearly 400 pages in this complete study, and yet there is so much more history that is exciting and helpful to know. At the end of this chapter, I will supply a list of suggested books for further reading. Lastly, let me plead with you as a Baptist minister who is burdened for his country and countrymen! God has used the Baptists to make this country what it is. I believe that with all my heart. Is that not what we would expect? The church ought to make the greatest contributions to any society or country. In light of this, I believe the Lord desires to use the Baptists once again. I beg of you, dear Baptist brethren, surrender all to God and let Him use you. Write your own chapter of faithful service and let God record it to challenge future generations that He may receive all the glory.

When I first began to study Baptist history, it was mostly exciting and new. It was a joy to learn of our rich heritage. After a while, God spoke to my heart with a sobering reminder, that, "…For unto whomsoever much is given, of him shall be much required…" (Luke 12:48b) and, "Therefore to him that knoweth to do good, and doeth *it* not, to him it is sin." (James 4:17). When we were ignorant of our history, we were in a bad place; however, to know it and not act upon it is the worst place of all. We must not let our study of Baptist heritage be merely educational. Let's stand together to believe God and serve God and surrender to God. Let's write the next chapter of Baptist history! And let's do it now!

Lesson Twelve

Suggested Further Reading

- *Trail of Blood,* J. M. Carroll
- *History of the Baptists,* J. T. Christian
- *America in Crimson Red,* James R. Beller
- *Sacred Betrayal,* James R. Beller
- *Israel of the Alps,* Alexis Muston
- *Baptist Foundations in the South,* William L. Lumpkin
- *Baptist Encyclopedia,* William Cathcart
- *This Day in Baptist History I & II,* David L. Cummins and E. Wayne Thompson
- *Baptist History Collection*** CD-ROM* (over 100 histories on one disc), the Baptist Standard Bearer, Inc.
- *Baptist Heritage Course, Vol. 1,* The Ancient Church, Ted Alexander
- *Baptist Heritage Conference Syllabus,* Ted Alexander

Review Questions

1. This is the lesson that teaches the student to _____ everything they have studied in their quest to know _____ _____.

2. Why should we suffer from the same _____ others have made?

3. If we apply the lessons we have learned from Baptist history, we will be _____ for it.

4. The Lord expects us to learn from the _____ and _____ of God's people in the past.

5. There has always been a _____ for liberty of conscience.

6. The _____ and their view of liberty are as corrupt as has ever been evidenced in history.

7. The Baptists are one of the only groups of people who have really _____ liberty.

8. Liberty of conscience is for _____.

9. The reformed groups reject _____ in part.

10. The Baptist worldview is one in which all men have a _____-_____ right to search the Scriptures for themselves and do with the _____ of the Bible what they choose.

11. Many Baptists today have been sucked into embracing the _____ worldview.

12. Once _____, the state holds great sway if a church wants out.

13. A state-church is a kind of _____ _____ that God never intended to exist!

14. Once liberty would be lost to a state-church of any kind, it would be nearly _____ to _____.

15. The influence Baptists have on civil government must be the kind of influence that transpires when men that fully _____ _____ are elected to office.

16. Baptists have always been strong _____ of the _____ of the local church.

17. It is abundantly evident that _____ abounded in and among the Baptists.

18. Our Baptist forebears were men of _____, doers and not _____ only.

19. The Separate Baptists of America were one of the most _____ _____ _____ in all of history.

20. The _____ ought to make the greatest contributions to any society or country. The Lord desires to use the _____ once again.

Answer Key

Lesson One
1. TAKEN
   GRANTED
2. IMMIGRANTS
3. BAPTISTS
4. LORD THEIR GOD
5. DEBT OF GRATITUDE
6. EUROPEAN BACKGROUND
7. CONTINUATION OF A LONG TIME
8. ENGLAND
9. RELIGIOUS DIRECTORS
   ENFORCERS
   PERSECUTORS
10. CONSCIENCES
11. HENRY VIII
12. ELIZABETH I
13. CHARLES I
14. MARY I
15. JAMES I
16. CHARLES I
17. FALSE
18. FALSE
19. FALSE
20. FALSE

Lesson Two
1. BAPTIST CHURCH
2. EVANGELISTIC REVIVAL

3. PORTSMOUTH
4. COLONIAL CHARTER
5. DEPUTY GOVERNOR
6. ACCOMPLISHMENTS
7. REVOLUTIONARY
   IMPOSSIBLE
8. ENGLAND
9. SCHOLAR
10. STUTTER
11. MAGISTRATE'S
    NON-APPROVED
12. ANTINOMIAN
13. NEW HAMPSHIRE
14. INFANT
15. STILLWELL'S
    LONDON, ENGLAND
16. JOHN CLARKE MEMORIAL
17. PROVIDENCE
18. FIRE-PROOF
19. THIRTEEN
20. EMINENT
BONUS: BENEFACTORS

Lesson Three
1. ENEMIES
2. PURITAN
   BAPTIST
3. PURIFY
   ENGLAND
4. GOVERNMENT
5. FIRST TABLE
6. SECOND TABLE

Answer Key

7. CALVINISTS
   COVENANT
8. WALL
   GARDEN
9. RELIGIOUS LIGHT
10. LIE
11. SEPARATION
12. CALVINISTS
    BIBLICAL BAPTIST
13. REMOVAL
    FEDERAL GOVERNMENT
14. CONGREGATIONAL
15. BAPTIST
    CLARKE
16. MEMBER
    BAPTIST CHURCH
17. BADGE
    WHORE
18. HATS
19. DEATH
20. YE HAVE BEATEN ME AS WITH ROSES

Lesson Four
1. AWAKENING
2. CONGREGATIONAL
3. HALFWAY
4. OLD ENGLAND
5. SEPARATE BAPTIST
   GREAT
6. EDWARD'S
7. HALFWAY COVENANT
8. BAPTISTS

       CALVAINISM
9.   CONTROVERSIE
10. OFTEN
       PRAYER
       SLEEP
11. SINNERS IN THE HANDS OF AN ANGRY GOD
12. GEORGE WHITEFIELD
13. ENGLISH LAD
14. BIBLE
       BROTHER
15. PEMBROKE
       OXFORD
16. JOHN
       CHARLES
17. WOMAN
       WELL
18. MAD
19. BIBLICAL/ANOINTED
20. MUST BE BORN AGAIN
21. FRANKLIN
       MILE
22. 175
23. CHICKENS
       DUCKS
24. SIX
       DOZEN
       NORTH CAROLINA
25. JOHN THE BAPTIST

Lesson Five
1.   HOLY GHOST

Answer Key

       PENTECOST
2. SANDY
       SHUBAL STEARNS
3. DEVIL
       BAPTISTS
4. AMERICA
5. CREEK
       WEEP
       CHURCHES
6. BOSTON
       1706
7. GEORGE WHITEFIELD
8. CHURCH
       NEW LIGHT
9. WAIT PALMER
10. TOLLAND
11. PASTOR WAIT PALMER
       PASTOR JOSHUA MORSE
12. HAMPSHIRE COUNTY, VIRGINIA
13. SIMPLE MEETING
14. SOUL-WINNERS
       BANNER
15. LANE
       DAVIS
16. SHOUTED
       REJOICED
17. SIXTEEN
       SIX HUNDRED
18. BIBLE BELT
       SEPARATE BAPTIST BELT
19. THIRTY
       SEVENTEEN

20. GEORGIA
21. REVEREND
    FATHER
22. APOSTLE
    ANGLICAN
23. 2,000
24. 65
25. CANNOT

Lesson Six
1. SPIRITUAL FABRIC
2. REVOLUTION
3. AMERICA
4. MILITARY
5. CIVIL
   RELIGIOUS
6. SUGAR
   STAMP
   TOWNSHEND
7. WILLIAM TRYON
8. HALF
9. REGULATORS
10. ALAMANCE
    MERRIL
11. SANDY CREEK, ABBOTTS CREEK, SHALLOW FORDS, DEEP CREEK, BELEW‚ÄÔS CREEK, HUNTING CREEK, AND JERSEY SETTLEMENT.
12. AMERICAN REVOLUTION
13. TYRANNY
14. CONGRESS
15. KING'S MOUNTAIN

16. BAPTIST
17. BAPTIZED
18. IMMERSION
19. AMERICAN IN CRIMSON RED
20. DEVIL

Lesson Seven
1. VIRGINIA
2. CHARLATANS
3. JOHN LELAND
4. RELIGIOUS
   POLITICAL
5. CONSCIENCE
6. JAMES MADISON
7. SALVATION
   SOUL
8. APOSTLE
   VIRGINIA
9. MURPHY BOYS
10. DANIEL MARSHALL
11. TONES
    GESTURES
12. SAMUEL HARRISS
13. TREMBLE
    REJOICE
14. SANG
    HYMN
15. DOWN HIS THROAT
16. PATRICK HENRY
17. 600
    600
    FOUR

18. EDINBURGH, SCOTLAND
19. SAMUEL HARRISS
20. FROM MY PALACE IN CULPEPPER
21. THE GUNPOWDER PLOT
    THE POISON PLOT
    THE SUFFOCATION PLOT
22. SWEARING JACK WALLER
23. KNIVES

Lesson Eight
1. MISSIONS
2. LONG TIME
3. FOREIGN MISSIONS
4. FLOUNDERED
5. ENGLAND
6. HYPER-CALVINISTS
7. JOHN GILL
8. CONVERT
   HEATHEN
9. EXTREMES
10. AMERICA
11. ATTEMPT
12. MODERN MISSIONS
13. PLEADING
    FOREIGN MISSIONS
14. FIVE
15. AMERICAN FOREIGN
16. BURMESE
17. PIONEERING STEPS
18. UNSUNG
19. BAPTIST HISTORY
20. DAVID BRAINERD

Answer Key

21. KENTUCKY
22. GREAT MOVE
23. MISSISSIPPI
    MISSOURI
24. KENTUCKY, INDIANA, OHIO, ILLINOIS, MICHIGAN, MISSOURI, KANSAS, NEBRASKA, OKLAHOMA
25. EXTINCTION

Lesson Nine

1. 1800
2. DEADNESS
3. SEVEN
4. GREAT AWAKENING
5. HOLY GHOST
   GOD
6. AMERICA
7. EMOTIONAL EXTREMES
8. PRESBYTERIANS
   METHODISTS
9. METHODIST
10. TAYLOR
11. SCRIPTURAL
12. PROMOTE
13. HEAVEN SENT
14. 326
15. 367
16. 5,310
17. 400
18. 1,802
19. 1802
20. 13,569

21. SPIRITUAL LANDSCAPE
22. GEORGIA
    VIRGINIA
23. 1815
24. KNEES
25. EXIST

Lesson Ten
1. MEN
2. PREACHER'S WIVES
3. VIRGINIA
4. 500
5. CHRISTIAN PROFESSORS
6. NASHVILLE
7. 150
   MEETING HOUSE
8. MISSOURI
9. 300
   8,000
10. 1,500
11. 2,000
12. ON HIM
13. A MILLION
14. BILLY GRAHAM
15. HYMN WRITER
16. DOCTRINAL
    BAPTIST
17. D.L. MOODY
18. ASHTABULA
19. COPYRIGHTED
20. PHILADELPHIA
21. FIVE

Answer Key

22. BROOKLYN, NEW YORK
23. DOANE
24. BRADBURY
25. JESUS LOVES ME

Lesson Eleven
1. EXTREME LEGALISM
2. SPLIT
3. CAME FROM
4. CONVICTION
   STAND
5. ADONIRAM
   CONGREGATIONALISTS
6. RICE
   TRIENNIAL
7. CENTRALIZED AUTHORITY
8. DENOMINATIONAL ORGANIZATION
9. NORTHERN
   SOUTHERN
10. SOUTH
11. SLAVERY
12. 1845
13. 1905
    ECCLESIOLOGY
14. BAPTIST BIBLE
15. FUNDAMENTAL BAPTIST FELLOWSHIP
16. AMERICAN BAPTIST CONVENTION
17. INDEPENDENT
18. BAPTISTS
19. NEW TESTAMENT
20. AFFILIATIONS
    IDENTIFICATION

DOCTRINE
PRACTICE

Lesson Twelve
1. APPLY
   BAPTIST HISTORY
2. MISTAKES
3. BETTER
4. SINS
   FAILURES
5. STRUGGLE
6. REFORMERS
7. UNDERSTOOD
8. EVERYONE
9. CATHOLICISM
10. GOD-GIVEN
    CHRIST
11. REFORMED
12. INCORPORATED
13. HYBRID MONSTER
14. IMPOSSIBLE
    RESTORE
15. UNDERSTAND LIBERTY
16. PROTECTORS
    ORDINANCES
17. CHARACTER
18. ACTION
    HEARERS
19. ZEALOUS EVANGELISTIC BODIES
20. CHURCH
    BAPTISTS